The Civil Service Competencies Book

Get a job in the Civil Service !

Second edition

Mike New

To my mother,
to whom I owe everything

Some material in this book also appears in The Competency Question Book for Job Interviews.

ISBN - 9781730951558

Contents

Chapter 1 What is a competency ?

1.1 What is a competency

A **competency** is simply a skill or an ability to do something efficiently. Don't be afraid of the word. Giving good service to a customer is a competency. Showing attention to detail is another. Problem-solving is another.

1.2 How competency recruitment works

Employment psychologists have told the Civil Service that competency recruitment is the best guide to how we would perform in any job. They believe that our past behaviour is a much more accurate guide to our future performance and therefore almost all interviews now are competency based. In both the application-form and the subsequent interview, you will be asked to give examples of how and when you demonstrated three or four particular skills.

Hundreds of people apply for just a handful of civil service and local government jobs. They cannot all be invited for an interview, so this method is used to select those applicants, who can demonstrate that they already have the required skills.

At this stage, many readers will already begin to feel anxious and start thinking that either they don't have the required abilities or else can't express them sufficiently well enough to convince the employer to recruit them. There are several reasons why people feel that way but it is mainly because most people are unaware of the skills they possess. I shall help you to evaluate yourself and to express all your many abilities in a strong, positive and persuasive manner.

I know that many people dread these type of questions and interviews. I meet them every day. However, to those who do dread them, I say : ' Have no fear ! ' From now on, I want you to change your mindset and to see them in a totally different light because they can be glorious opportunities.

1.3 The advantages to you of competency applications

How many times do you encounter job adverts that strictly require certain qualifications ? Or so many years similar experience already within that role ? They are very disheartening. Competency applications give you the opportunity to really sell your talents and your worth to an employer. If you have done the job or done the task or something similar to what you are being asked about, then the employer is willing to overlook any lack of qualifications that you may have. Employers are now more interested in what you have done, not who you are or how much you have managed to memorise for exams.

Another great advantage is that, unless the interviewer specifically asks you for an example from work, you can relate an example from any sphere of your life. It might be a group you are involved in, a neighbourhood activity or some voluntary work you once did. It might be an experience you once had while on holiday. If you can show qualities of great leadership, it doesn't matter whether you demonstrated them at school or amongst friends at weekends or on holiday or in a previous job. Although it is better if you can narrate an example of a competency in a similar employment situation, you may use examples of your skills from any area of your life.

You might have noticed that on the inside cover of this book, I wrote "No qualifications needed". It's true. Civil Service recruiters are more interested in your skills than your qualifications. George Osborne was the Chancellor of the Exchequer, running the economy of this country and in charge of trillions and yet he didn't even have a GCSE in Economics or Business Studies. This point is very important and I shall be saying a lot more about this later.

Yet another advantage is that you can prepare your answers in advance. Many people hated the old situational interviews, where you were suddenly given a hypothetical scenario and asked to imagine what you would do. Often, jobseekers had never encountered that situation before in their lives and the experience was really stressful. You can take your time and carefully prepare your answers , at your leisure , without being under the hot spotlight of an interview and having to answer stressful questions. You can prepare your answers and practise them over and over again.

From this moment onwards, you must drop your dread of competency interviews. Don't fight the fear, just drop it. It will smash on the floor. If you follow my guidelines and are willing to work hard, you will be in a much better position and actually look forward to showcasing your skills at such interviews ! You will build up your own Experiences Autobiography and have a bagful of confidence.

Summary of advantages :

The employer will overlook the lack of any paper qualifications
You can relate examples from any area of your life
You can carefully prepare your examples in advance

Chapter 2 The Answer Format

2.1 The application-form will look something like this ......

Competency examples

Tell us about a time you have demonstrated the relevant knowledge, experience or skills for each required competency.

Delivering at pace

Give an example of when you have demonstrated this competency
Not to exceed 250 words

Word count 0

2.2 You will need to type your answer in Microsoft Word or similar, perform a spellcheck and then a word count on it (it's on the 'Review' tab in Word) and then Copy & Paste it into the answer-box.

2.3 Using the CAR format to answer

Your answer must be structured in a certain way : it must have three distinct stages. You must describe the C**ircumstance** of a particular situation or problem that needed resolving, then the A**ction** you took to resolve it and finally what the R**esult** and benefits were. Now read that again because it is very, very important. Fail to grasp it and you will certainly fail to get an interview.

Using the following simple format ensures that your story has a logical flow.

C stands for Circumstance

Firstly, you will set the scene by describing the **CIRCUMSTANCE.** This is telling the interviewer what the situation or problem was that needed your attention. It is putting things in context. You will need to ask yourself : What was the situation ? What was the task you faced ? What was the problem that needed solving ? How did it arise or how you get to be given it ?

A stands for Action

Next, you will describe what **ACTION** you took to remedy the problem. This is where you go into the specifics and spell out exactly what you did and it gives you the opportunity to sell yourself to the employer. This is where you demonstrate how you have the competency which is being sought in the job advert. You tell how you have already successfully dealt with this situation in the past. You must detail not only what action you took but what skills you employed.

When preparing to write this, you will need to ask : What action did you take and why ? Were there several approaches you could have adopted ? If so, why did you elect to take the one you did ? What skills did you use which demonstrate the competency exactly ? Show the steps you took and any difficulties you faced. How did you overcome them ? If people resisted you, how did you counter their objections ?

Wherever possible, try to choose an example which is as similar as possible to the job for which you are now applying. Wherever possible, try to demonstrate that you have already done exactly what the interviewer is asking or something similar.

R stands for Result

Finally, you summarise the **RESULT**, stating how you completed the task and detailing the benefits to you, your employer, your team or customers. If possible, quantify your success with hard figures. Don't say " I made my company a lot of money. " Instead, you must say " I increased turnover by 5%, which equated to £20,000 per year." Or : " I saved my employer 7% on his stationery charges, which equated to £800 per year". If you cannot provide hard figures, then quote any praise or positive feedback you received from customers, colleagues or your Team Leader or any bonus or rewards.

Approximately 10 % of your time should be spent setting the scene, 75% describing the action that you took and 15% describing the result.

2.4 Here is an example of an answer to Competency 3 : Making effective decisions

" Using sound judgement, evidence and knowledge to arrive at accurate, expert and professional decisions and advice".

You are asked to give an example of when you have made an effective decision and how you went about it.

Your answer :

> Realising I needed a computer at home, I was unsure whether to buy a PC or a laptop. It was a major expenditure and I had to get it right.
>
> The first thing I did was I identified my specific objective (buy a computer) and my specific needs - immediate, medium and long term. I questioned myself as to its primary purpose - writing ? music ? family webchats ? How much speed and storage would I need and how soon would it be obsolete? I then collected as much relevant information as I needed, from a wide variety of sources, ensuring the info was up-to-date (- brochures in shops, websites, chatrooms, consumer groups, independent reviews). I then consulted with computer-shop assistants, friends and work colleagues for advice.
>
> After organising the material in a way that would help analysis and extracting the relevant info appropriately, I generated realistic options for my budget, which led me to decide on a laptop. I filtered the options to a shortlist of three (based on spec, length of guarantee, I.T support and price). After assessing the pros, cons and risks of each and confirming my understanding (by emailing the companies), I then made my decision based on evidence.
>
> The outcome was that I bought a laptop which served my needs and budget perfectly, improved my productivity and passed all my quality control criteria. I later saw that model go on to win many awards.

240 words.

There are a number of things to be noticed from that example, which I will examine later but for now, just see how the structure follows the **C.A.R** format. The circumstance is briefly explained , then the action you took to deal with the situation is narrated and takes up the bulk of the example and then the positive outcome is given. All within 250 words.

It is imperative that you adhere strictly to this C.A.R format or you will surely fail.

Chapter 3 Your Experiences Autobiography

3.1 The experience stocktake

One of the greatest difficulties that jobseekers face with competency application forms is that they cannot think of a specific example of when they have performed that competency and cannot describe an occasion when they have demonstrated their skills in that area. It is highly frustrating for them because they know that they have performed that action to a high standard before but cannot recall it on demand. They lose the job of their dreams. Is this you ?

If you already have great examples of your skills then you probably don't need this book. Most people don't have examples, so how are you going to get them ? You will get them by going backwards in your life to make yourself aware of all the experiences you have had. To do this, I am going to get you to realise and recognise that you possess many more skills than you may realise. I want you to do **an experience stocktake**.

This book is not going to give you answers on a plate , which you can simply 'Copy & Paste' onto your application-form. Life isn't like that. The answers given in later chapters are simply examples which show you the standard required and the format you will need to structure your answers.

Sofia worked in a call-centre. I asked her to list her duties. She replied: " *I just answered incoming calls from people, who had seen adverts in papers. I took their details and arranged for info to be sent out to them* ".

Actually, what she did was to deliver excellent customer service in a friendly and professional manner by taking incoming calls . She would use her great communication skills to actively listen and communicate appropriately and sometimes employ her persuasion and business acumen skills to sell additional items. She would use her time management skills to control talkative callers and meet her targets and her negotiation skills and problem-solving skills to sort out any callers who phoned in with complaints. She often exchanged her shift days with colleagues, showing her teamwork nature. She would log the confidential details of callers onto the inhouse software , while still actively listening, demonstrating her multi-tasking ability and IT skills.

Can you see that whilst Sofia thought that she only answered calls, took details and arranged for items to go out, she actually has a broad range of skills that she can use as starting points for examples in an interview situation ? This is so typical. Most people do not realise that they have many skills until they are pointed out to them or are forced to sit and evaluate themselves. They must do an Experiences Stocktake to realise and categorise all their skills, so that is what we will do now.

3.2 List your duties in detail

Now comes the hard work. This chapter demands a great deal of work from you but I make no apology for that. Nothing in life is free. The rewards will be worth it.

I am going to make you remember and record all your experiences and compile them into your own **Experiences Autobiography**.

If you are currently working, I want you to list what you did in your job last week, **in detail.** Every duty you had to perform, no matter how small or trivial it may seem. If last week was not a typical week because you were on a training course for example, then use a typical week. List all the people you liaised with, both inside your workplace and outside. List any incidents . List all the equipment / machinery you used. That is very important. List every function you performed, even the smallest. Why ? Because every experience you have had could help you to land that job you seek. The purpose of this is to get you to ultimately see that **you have many more abilities than you realise** and have had many more experiences than you think.

Let me explain. Josh was an office worker and wondered at first why I was asking him to list the office machinery he used. It then prompted him to remember that the fax/ photocopier had a paperjam last week. That in turn reminded him about the time last year when he was alone because everyone was out to lunch and the fax/photocopier had jammed and he had a really urgent fax to send and how he was in a real mess. He decided not to panic.

He stayed calm and considered all his options. He thought about it for a few moments. He remembered that there was a manual in the fax drawer. He looked and found it wasn't there. He stayed calm and thought again. He copied down the name and model number of the machine, searched for it in Google, found the manual online, followed the trouble-shooting diagrams and quickly found the solution. So, he then realised that he did have problem-solving skills after all and had an example that he could use in any competency interview. He could also use that experience as an ' Initiative' example.

You must understand that all our experiences in life are important and that we forget most of them. Your task over the coming days and weeks is to try to remember those experiences and list them. From now on, you must get into the habit of recording your experiences in your **Experiences Autobiography**. More about that later .

So, list EVERY action that you performed last week in your job, however small.

- Whom did you communicate / meet with ? Inside or outside the job.
- Did you work with others in any way ? Teamworking skills ?
- Did you perform a service of any kind whatsoever ?
- Did you have any deadlines or targets to meet ? Daily ? Monthly ?
- Did you achieve anything ?
- Did you solve any problems ? Not a single one ?
- Did you resolve any disputes ?
- Did you organise anything ?
- Did you create anything ?
- Did you manage anything ?
- Did you improve, innovate, suggest anything ?
- Did you show flexibility or adapt to changes or new working practices ?
- Overcome setbacks or obstacles ?
- Did you negotiate ? Did you persuade ?
- Make any major decisions ?
- Plan something ? Take responsibility for something ?
- Give a presentation ? A speech ?
- Take the initiative ?
- Motivate someone ?
- Save the company any money or save waste ?
- Use any equipment ?

Think very slowly and carefully and take your time. This exercise must not be rushed or omitted. Don't be lazy. Invest time in this and you will be very surprised at what you find. A small experience can often spark a memory of something which can give you an excellent competency example.

If you do not have a job at the moment, then list all the things you did in your last two jobs. Remember to write down even the smallest thing you did. All the people you spoke to, inside and outside the company. All the equipment you used. All the incidents.

<u>If you are a school-leaver</u> or have never worked, no problem ! This next part applies to you too.

3.3 Now list every job you have ever done

Now comes the really hard work ! I want you to do the same for **all your previous** jobs. Yes, that's right, every single one. Seriously. Even if all your previous jobs have been in the same line of work, there will have been incidents that provide examples that can be used in your interview. The challenge now is for you to dig through your memory and exhume those long forgotten experiences and achievements. They can prove to be very valuable. The more time and effort you invest in remembering your past experiences, the far easier it will be to demonstrate your skills to an employer and land that dream job. It's that simple.

Ask your family and friends for help ! Ask you family, friends, partner, relatives and colleagues to remind you of all your previous jobs and things that have happened to you in the past. Log them all. For now, in no particular order.

3.4 List any of these achievements or activities :

School - Attended all year round - you never missed a day ? Head boy ? One of the house captains ? Any special responsibility ? In drama society ? In debating team ? In choir ? Best achiever of the Year ? Won the cross country county race ? Team sports captain ? It's unlikely that you would be asked to prove these by the interviewer but it will show the interviewer what type of person you are, what you achieved and can form the basis of other examples. Even being in the choir shows you can work in a team.

Scouts / Girl Guides / St John's Ambulance Brigade - Any notable achievements ? Have you raised any money for charity ? Saved a life ?

Part-time jobs while at school - Paper boy. Milk boy. Cleaner. Saturday job helping in a shop, yard, garage, market stall or farm. Note : no job is worthless. Every job is useful and has dignity and value, if done well, even the most humble.

Voluntary work or charity work - Shopped for the elderly ? Decorated an old folks' flat ? Mowed their lawn ? Shovelled their snow away ? Raised money ? Looked after a pet ? Did a charity sponsored run/ marathon /walk ? Served in a second-hand shop ? Acted as a delivery driver for a charity shop ? Drive anyone home ? Served meals to the homeless at Christmas ? Handed out food at a food bank ? Organise a food bank ? Did anything happen ?

Community work Organised a fireworks party for your street ? Organised or helped to run any sort of community party / celebration / commemoration for your block of flats, street or community ? Anything happen ? Acted as chairman, treasurer, minutes-taker or in any capacity in any neighbourhood watch / security scheme ? Act as a local spokesperson or representative ?

Church work Assisted in any way at your local church ? Helped organise or run annual fete ? Helped run the food bank ? Visited the elderly or sick ?

Local sports club Washed their kit ? Designed their leaflets ? Coached the kids ? Raised money for them ? Organised raffles bingos for them ? Worked in a team to clear snow off the pitch ?
Neighbours Solved disputes between them ? Done favours for them ? Communicated on their behalf ? Worked as a team with them ? Organised a street party or fireworks party ?
Local hospital - Ever helped it ? Attended their fete ? What happened ? Ever been a patient ? Made arrangements ? Visited the sick as a volunteer visitor ?
Local old cinema / concert hall - Ever tried to save it from closure ?
Olympic torch - Did you carry it ? What happened ?
In a hobbies club : chess, gardening. reading, inventing, computing, archery, cooking ? What happened ? Did you organise any competitions ? work as teams ? any accidents happen ? Resolve any problems or disputes ?
Travel experiences - see a crime ? negotiate a better deal ? have to change to a different hotel or airport ? get lost ? miss a flight ? give English lessons for free board or food ? prevent an accident ? had to hitch-hike ? get mugged or held up at gun-point ?
Health club / Gym Motivated yourself ? Lost weight ?
Evening-classes - Taken courses to improve your skills or health ?
Driving test - any incidents ? Make any sacrifices to pay for your lessons ?
Wedding - **B**est man duties ? Give a speech ?
Holidays - **P**lanned any ? Organised any ? Actions abroad.
Family jobs with your children or nephews / nieces / grandchildren - Things you've done with kids : Organised birthday parties. Organised days out.
Any internships, work experience, placements, training courses, job-shadowing, school / uni coursework or fieldwork ?

Dig out all your old payslips and diaries to remind you of your previous jobs. Find all certificates of achievements, accolades, awards, school reports, letters of promotion and qualifications. All of these are vital reminders of your experiences and skills.

3.5 A CV warning. If you have already compiled a CV, don't be tempted to just copy the duties you have written on it ,thinking that is sufficient and that you can omit the above exercise. A CV is merely a brief skeleton of your past. I want you to spend a good deal of time painstakingly reminding yourself of every single task you have ever done. If it takes you a week, then so be it. I cannot emphasise enough the importance of this exercise.

3.6 Building your Experiences Autobiography

The next step is to buy an A4 pad and a hard folder for it. On the front of the folder, write in a permanent black pen ' **Experiences Autobiography** '. .Alternatively, if you can afford to buy a large hardback notebook, whose pages have already been subdivided from A to Z, then so much the better.

The task now is to transfer your past experiences into your Experiences Autobiography by categorising them in a way which will assist you in getting your next job.

At the top of the page of your A4 pad, write the following competencies, one on each sheet :

- Attention to Detail and Quality Assurance - accuracy and standards
- Change - adaptability, flexibility and versatility
- Commercial instinct – how you have made or saved money
- Communication Skills - Verbal, written or phone skills
- Deadlines, Targets and Achieving including Time Management
- Decision Making and Problem Solving
- Drive, Determination and Resilience, including Self-motivation
- Equality and Diversity
- Initiative
- Leadership
- Negotiation, Persuasion , Influence and Motivating Others
- Self-improvement - training
- Teamwork – collaborating and partnering

You should have a separate sheet for each competency.

If you are using an A-Z notebook, obviously, you would enter *Teamwork* under T, *Attention to Detail* under A , etc.

3.7 Logging your experiences into competencies

So, here is an example of how you must log all your past experiences into your Experience Autobiography file or book. Peter is an 18 year-old school-leaver who has not worked full-time but has remembered that he worked as a paper-boy and on one occasion, he noticed a man lying on the floor in his hallway.

He looked through the letter-box and realised that something was seriously wrong, went to the next-door neighbour and had him call an ambulance. His quick thinking saved that man's life. So, under the competency sheet headed ' *Initiative*', he writes ' Paperboy job – called ambulance' and writes the same under 'Leadership', since he took control of the situation. That will remind him of that situation. While he was doing that job, he also had to interact with his customers, so he writes ' Paperboy job ' on his ' *Communication* ' sheet.

When he was in the 6th form, he was part of a group that were given a day's instruction in decorating and then volunteered to decorate a pensioner's flat. They had to complete it in four days. So, he wrote ' Decorated pensioner's flat ' under the following competency categories : *Deadlines, Targets and Achieving; Attention to Detail and Teamwork.* That one experience can serve as 3 competency examples.

John is 19. He has had one part-time job and one full-time job. When at school, he had a Saturday job washing cars. It did not involve meeting the customers but he did have to wash so many cars per hour and to a high standard. So, he writes Washed Cars under the competency category *Deadlines, Targets and Achieving* and also again under *Attention to Detail.* He had a full-time temporary job as a Mailroom Assistant in a team with an Insurance Company. So, he enters 'Mailroom Assistant ' under the *Teamwork* ' category. He remembers that the job involved carefully weighing the post and calculating the correct postage of envelopes and packages. So, he enters Mailroom Assistant Weighing under ' *Attention to Detail* '. He remembers that he had to liaise with the staff on all floors, taking their instructions and also receiving post from couriers . He enters 'Mailroom Liaison with staff and couriers' under the *Communication* competency. Since he had strict time deadlines each day to meet , he notes that under the *Deadlines, Targets and Achieving* competency.

Finally, since the job had its ups and downs in volumes of work due to mailshots , TV ads, etc, he had to be flexible over shifts, staying late and working overtime. He writes ' Required overtime at Mail job' under the *Change, Flexibility and Adaptability* category.

The more examples you build up, the easier it becomes to complete the application-forms. I cannot emphasise that enough.

3.8 Do you get the idea ?

If John now applies for a job which has a competency interview and the interviewer asks him for examples of when he has ever had to pay attention to detail or work in a team or communicate with others or work to a deadline or be flexible at work, he has ready- made examples in his Experiences Autobiography. .

He has these examples because he has taken the time and trouble to think exactly and specifically of the actions he has done in the past, to write them down and then to assign them to one or more competencies. That is your challenge. The reward is a good job. Now do it !

3.9 If you are returning to work after a long time away from the workplace

If you are perhaps a parent or a carer who has been at home for some years and are now trying to get back into the world of work which is different from the equally demanding world of housework and caring, you will need to give examples of your behaviours which meet the required competencies.

Although returning to work can seem daunting, don't worry : millions have achieved it and so can you. Firstly, the Civil Service is equally accepting of examples from outside the workplace. Secondly, you can easily build up a strong Experiences Autobiography with valid , excellent examples of your competence and skills by realising that what you have done in the home and with others are " transferable skills" . All you need is to get into the habit of closely identifying your actions.

For example, if you are asked in an interview for an example of how you have organised, you can state how you have organised your child's birthday party or playgroups or arranged babysitters or planned ahead for your child's new term. You have organised your time effectively so that all the washing, cleaning, ironing, shopping, school runs, visits to doctors and chemists and all meals are prepared on time and kids are bathed all on time. You know how much organising that takes so don't let others underestimate it.

If asked for an example of your **delivering at pace,** you would tell of how you got all your kids to school on time each day, how you budgeted perfectly and how you paid all your bills perfectly without incurring any penalties. You budgeted ahead for birthdays, bills and emergencies too.

For examples of your response to **change,** you often had to adapt to unexpected circumstances, such as when your kids became ill, were sent home from school (teachers on strike, school snowed off,),your kids had accidents and you found a solution to the problem.

Communication skills ? You have had to deal with the teachers and PTA, the council, the Benefits Agency . You can mention the other groups you may be part of, including online forums.

Determination and resilience ? Describe how you stuck up for your child's rights through thick and thin in a prolonged struggle with the Education Department or school or how you won a long benefit claim for the person for whom you were caring.

Mothers will certainly have no difficulty citing examples of **achieving commercial outcomes** and **getting value for money** . It's something you have had to do every day.

You will need to persuade prospective employers that the life skills you have developed over the years – and they are indeed valuable and considerable - are relevant to them and to the advertised job.

To do this, you will need to examine every single action you have taken while you have been out of the workplace. Yes, I know it is a laborious job but nothing comes easy to us in life and you will ultimately be rewarded if you do so. Write all your experiences into your **Experiences Autobiography**, as I have described.

3.10 If you are a young person with very little work experience

Don't despair. The same applies to you as to the members of the group in 3.9 You too can build up an Experiences Autobiography by relating all your school experiences and all the experiences with friends, on holidays, in various groups and in the community – even in online groups and friendships – as examples of your skills. You can even use experiences with your family members or friends. These are just as valid.

For example, when asked for examples of **Adapting to Change,** you can say how you adapted to a new home / teacher /6th form/ step-parent/ baby sibling/ the loss of someone or any sudden change, welcome or otherwise. Don't worry. The details I've given for each competency later in the book will help you describe how you did it.

Attention to Detail / Quality Assurance – Any Maths, Science or Computing students should have no difficulty narrating how their equations or formulae had to be exact in order to balance or how their computer program they had coded had to be without a single error in order to run. Any Social Sciences students can state how they had to ensure their data was accurate. History students can say their dates had to perfect and Literature students can say their quotations had to be verbatim.

For **Communication** examples, you can state you can state how you had to carefully structure your essays : the need to plan them, to have a brief intro of a couple of sentences, a main body of two or three paragraphs where it develops and then a final paragraph where you summarise it all and perhaps state your conclusion. You might remember how you had to give a small speech or presentation to your class on your coursework or how you explained the internet or mobile phones or Skype to elderly people.

For examples of **Delivering at Pace / working to Deadlines and Targets**, you might care to mention how you prioritised your assignments / essays/ coursework and exam preparation by deciding what was Urgent, what was Important and which was Non-urgent and allowing Contingency Time for any emergencies. Note the specific examples and of how you organised things. Tell how you never failed to submit your work on time and never felt too rushed because you planned well.

For **Decision Making**, stick with how you went about selecting your options or choosing your college or uni. State how you went about your decision. Remember to say you based it on data /evidence not emotion.

For **Drive, Determination and Resilience,** maybe you passed your exams after recovering from a bad accident or a family bereavement or divorce. Maybe you lost weight or eventually managed to run a half-marathon or ride 40 miles on your bike after several attempts. The point is that you persevered and didn't give up. Show them that.

For **Teamworking** examples, you can narrate how you participated in a team project, perhaps how you contributed computer code or some ideas. Remember that you can use any experiences from outside of school, so tell of how you help the neighbourhood / community team clear up litter from the street / park / woods. Perhaps you played in a team, even an online one. That is valid too.

A prospective employer is willing to accept all and any of your examples , if they are well prepared and you can show him that your past behaviour matches what he is looking for. Believe me, you can do it. Many have done it with my help and YOU can too. The Prime Minister , the President of the USA and the Pope had not done the job before but all had done something a bit similar. That's all you need.

Ask your family and friends for help if you are stuck for ideas. Any experiences you have had count. The times you have helped your uncle or neighbour on his market stall at weekends can provide just about any competency. Think hard and remember !

Chapter 4 How to answer competency questions Part 2

4.1 Your next step is to carefully read each of the competencies stated on the application-form, for which you will need to provide an example. Then, you will look through your Experiences Autobiography and find experiences which match and which can be used as your answers.

4.2 Using an experience creatively

It's important to realize that an experience can be used to answer several competencies. Remember Josh in Chap. 3.2, who sent the urgent fax ? He could use that experience to answer both a Problem-Solving question which was thrown at him or an Initiative question. If someone had worked on a helpdesk in a supermarket, answering customer enquiries, they could use that experience for any Problem-Solving, Communication or Teamwork question. If you had worked shifts on a till in a shop, you could use that as an example for Attention to Detail/Quality or Change or Communication. If you had taken on that job after suffering a major setback in your life such as a bereavement or separation or illness, then you also use it for Delivering at Pace. Be careful about using illness however, unless it was just an accident, as employers generally do not like to hear about illness.

4.3 Match your example to the job

When you look through your Autobiography, it is important to try to use an experience which matches the duties of the job as well as the competency question, as closely as possible. Re-read the job advert again to see exactly what you would be doing on a daily basis.

If you have three or four examples of when you worked as a good teamworker, use the one which most closely matches the duties of the job in question. Answer in a way that brings benefit to the employer.

4.4 Writing your examples

You have identified experiences which you can use for your examples. Hopefully, you will have several for each competency. Don't panic if you have only one or none at this moment. Choose the strongest and most relevant example you have. The next step is to expand your rough example into a draft answer.

You are required to answer in no more than 250 words and this can be really challenging. It seems as if the Civil Service HR staff have just plucked this arbitrary figure out of thin air, since they expect you to set the context of a situation, describe in detail how you successfully resolved a difficult problem and outline the benefits, all within just 250 words ! Even worse, you are sometimes expected to demonstrate more than one competency within that limit. It is nonsense but we have to deal with the confines of that figure until common sense is restored.

Since you are going to have to pack in a lot of info, I would advise you to aim for somewhere around either 12 sentences of 20 words each or else 16 sentences of 15 words each. Both total 240 words. For some, it will be difficult to fit everything in and they will be using the '&' symbol for 'and' and using their thesaurus often. In time, you will eventually become skilled at editing your story to fit.

4.5 You are expected to boast !

In our normal life, we are taught not to boast . It is frowned upon and we isolate people who do it. However, there is one exception in life when boasting is not only acceptable but expected and that is in an interview. You must absolutely tell the interviewer how capable you are because you only have this one opportunity. He is not a mind reader. He cannot know your abilities. You must spell them out for him. You must boast about your skills and achievements, not about YOU. Say that you are proud of having achieved XYZ , not because you are brilliant but because you worked extremely hard or you made many sacrifices or overcame many obstacles to get it. I want you ,right now, to change your mindset about any reservation or shyness you have about boasting. Believe me - it is expected in an interview. Don't let that precious opportunity pass you by. It might not come again. The employer wants to hear how good you are !

4.6 Using effective, descriptive action words

When writing your scripts, it is important to use specific, descriptive action words which tell the employer exactly what you did. It is not enough to keep saying " I did this and then I did that and then I did something else."

If you are giving an example of ' Attention to Detail/Quality ', it sounds far better to say " I carefully monitored the dials" rather than " I checked the dials." If you were answering an ' Initiative ' question, it's better to say that you "pre-empted a potentially serious accident in the workplace " rather than you stopped someone slipping on water. When giving an example of ' Value for Money' you told how you noticed part of the procedure was no longer necessary so you streamlined it. That sounds much better than " I cut parts out ". Employers like to hear " streamlined", since it suggests a saving of their money. You will find a list of action words to use in Chapter 6. Add your own words to the list as you go along but ensure you know the correct meaning of a word before using it. Use the words for accuracy, not for ego.

4.7 A sample answer of Competency 2 - Changing and Improving

"People who are effective n this area take initiative, are innovative and seek out opportunities to create effective change. It's about learning from what has worked well and what hasn't; being open to change and improvement; working 'smarter', in more focused ways ".

"Give an example of when you have been adaptable to change "

Now for an example. Mark has read a job advert. It requires him to give an example of Competency 2, Changing and Improving. He looks through his Experiences Autobiography and he finds an example of when he worked for local government in the public transport section and when he was suddenly told that he would have to work in the Information Unit the following week to cover sickness absence. He had only ever been shown around there once before and knew that there was IT and switchboard which was unfamiliar to him .

He knew none of the staff and knew that the place was manically busy. His usual job was giving out info to the public face-to-face but he was suddenly going to have to adapt to working in a very busy call-centre environment , something he had never done before.

The challenge for Mark now is to script this in a way that he will be able to demonstrate how he has coped with change in a very positive manner. He will write his script and probably change it a few times until he is happy with it. He will read it to friends and family and get their feedback. Here is his answer :

A sample answer :

In the council's Transport department, I sold tickets to the public and answered enquiries. One Thursday, my Team Leader told me that on Monday, I would be needed in the Information Unit. It was a call-centre environment, containing a large switchboard and a lot of I.T I was unfamiliar with.

So, I adopted a positive approach to the change, seeing it as an opportunity to acquire more skills and efficient working practices. I asked my Team Leader if I could spend some time the next day at the Information Unit, familiarising myself with the equipment and acquainting myself with the staff and layout. She agreed and I spent the Friday there, learning as much as I could.

I liaised with many external partners such as the Police, Coastguard, Emergency Services, the Press, the utility companies etc. I familiarised myself with the tech and even the canteen, toilets and my own route there, so as minimize the strangeness the following week.

The result was that on the Monday, I hit the ground running. Those two weeks were pressurised but because I had planned the change and managed it, it had been a disruption to me but not an upheaval. I had learned new switchboard skills too , which I added to my CV. The Team Leader of the Information Unit was so impressed that he asked me to join his team permanently. I had decided to be the manager of the change, not its victim ."

Firstly, notice how he went by car : he used the C.A.R format. He briefly explained the circumstance (the background, the context) , he then told what action he took and he finally told of a successful outcome. It is imperative that you use this format. Some people elsewhere have suggested using S.T.A.R (Situation, task, Action, Result) but why unnecessarily complicate matters ?

Secondly, in the following chapters, I have listed the essential indicators for each competency and what you must do is to incorporate some of these into your answer. So, in this particular example, Mark wrote " adopted a positive approach", "saw it as an opportunity to learn more skills", " planned the change" " made full use of new tech", "managed the change".

In other words, he used words and phrases which all show that he was adaptable and flexible to the process of change. He managed and planned his two week disruption in advance, rather than reacting to it.

Thirdly, notice that he used "I " throughout the narrative, not “we”. The employer is not interested in what others have done in the past but in what YOU have done in the past. There are rules you must follow when writing your answer and I have compiled them in a list for you in Chapter 5. It is vital that you use that checklist before submitting your answers.

Fourthly, notice that he explained what he had learned and how he had benefited from the experience. He ended the story positively and powerfully, both in saying that the Unit's Team Leader tried to headhunt him and also repeating a memorable slogan. It is essential to state the benefits achieved to your employer or to you or your team by your actions.

In later examples, you will see that it is always best of all to quantify that success in terms of hard figures, if possible. Don’t say “ I ended up saving my boss a lot of money “ but “ My proposals resulted in a saving of 5%, which equated to £20,000 per year”.

You will not get your script right the first time and will have to amend it several times before you are happy with it.

4.8 Writer’s block

There are usually two main stumbling blocks in writing examples : the first is choosing the right experience that you will use for your example and the second is getting bogged down in actually writing it.

Take your time choosing your example and choose the one which most closely matches the description by the Civil Service for that competency. If you are facing writer’s block and just cannot get your idea onto paper, then break it down into small, bite-size chunks. Roughly jot down the C.A and R and then write out the C (Circumstance) part first and then have a little break. Then do the Action part and take another break before doing the Result part.

4.9 Keep your examples

When you are happy with your example, having perhaps tried it out in front of family or friends, put it in your Experiences Autobiography. Hopefully, it will help you to land this job and then you will not need again for a long time but do keep it, to save you having to write it again.

4.10 If you can't think of any examples

If you have really spent time looking back at all the experiences in your life, both in work and outside, as I have described in chapter 2 and you have looked at the examples given under the competencies in chapters 7 and 8 and you still can't think of any examples of things you have done which match the competencies in the job advert, then I would suggest that the job may not be right for you. Listen to your heart. It is the best guide. Unless you are reaching out for a radically different change of career, it seems that you could well be going for a job that might be unsuitable for you. Are you sure you want to do this ? You can never be happy unless you are true to yourself. Follow your own inner nature, no matter what. There are too many square pegs in round holes. You will never be happy in life until you find the right hole for yourself.

4.10 Checking your example

- Is most of your answer taken up by your ACTION ?
- Have you included everything ?
- Have you repeated yourself by accident ?
- Have you mostly spoken about what YOU did ?
- Have you given an example similar to the job you are now applying for ?
- Have you described the benefits to you or the team or company or customer and if appropriate, been able to QUANTIFY them with hard figures and percentages ?
- Have you said what you learned from the experience ?
- Have you **finished with a strong impact** , that the employer will remember ?

Chapter 5 What to do and what not to do

THINGS YOU MUST DO :

- ✓ Use the C.A.R format – Circumstance, Action, Result.
- ✓ Use examples from any area of your life.
- ✓ Have more than one example prepared for each competency
- ✓ Try to choose an example which matches the duties in the job description and the grade, as much as possible
- ✓ Tell in specifics what you did, relating your actions to the competency indicators and to THIS job.
- ✓ Talk about what YOU did, not what others did.
- ✓ Detail HOW you achieved it and how you overcame any objections, setbacks and obstacles
- ✓ Convey as much information in the shortest possible time, emphasising key skills.
- ✓ QUANTIFY your success with figures and stats. If not, say you were praised by your supervisor or colleagues or customers.
- ✓ Boast about your skills, not about you. Say your achievements are due to hard work and sacrifice, just as much as your skills.
- ✓ Stay focused on the question.
- ✓ Keep within the 250 word limit
- ✓ Ensure your example has a happy ending !
- ✓ Finish with a strong impact and with you being praised

THINGS YOU MUST NOT DO :

x **Don't assume** that the interviewer knows the background. Carefully but briefly set the context.

x **Don't generalise** : e.g. Don't say "I'm always polite to customers " The interviewer is not interested in how you normally are. He wants an example of what you have done already , which shows that skill.

x **Don't give a job description** : e.g Don't say "My job involves" or " I do this ." The interviewer is simply not interested in what your job involves. He wants an example of what you've done.

x **Don't theorize** : e.g Don't say "Well, I would / I generally / I tend to ." The interviewer is not interested in what you would do. He wants an example of what you have done in the past which demonstrates that particular competency.

x **Don't assert** : e.g Don't say " It is very important to..(get along with your colleagues"). The interviewer is not interested in your assertions. He wants to hear an example of when you have done which shows that particular ability.

x **Don't depersonalise it** : e.g Don't use 'We' Don't tell what others did. Tell what **YOU** did, not what others did . Use **" I ",** not " We **".**

x **Don't blind him with science** : He might not know the technicalities of your job. Keep it simple.

x **Don't use jargon**, abbreviations or slang. Don't assume the interviewer will understand your private language.

x **Don't be unbalanced.** Remember : most of the time should be spent on describing the **ACTION** you took.

x **Don't malign anyone.** Don't criticize customers, your past or current interviewers or your colleagues.

x **Don't use controversial subjects as examples.** Stay with safe topics.

x **Don't try to come across as Superman** : the examples don't have to be extraordinary. You don't need to have invented a new gadget or saved your boss a million pounds. Just come across as being very good at your job.

- **Don't waffle.** Be concise and crisp. Don't beat about the bush. Stay sharply focused.

Chapter 6 Action Words to Use

When writing your answers and when in the interview, use these words to describe the actions you took :

I achieved
I adapted
I adopted
I analysed
I arranged
I assessed
I built
I combined
I compiled
I completed
I conducted
I controlled
I considered
I consulted
I coordinated
I created
I delivered
I designed
I developed
I devised
I diagnosed
I directed
I eliminated
I enabled
I encouraged
I ensured
I established
I exceeded
I expanded
I extracted
I evaluated
I evolved
I fostered
I furthered
I gained
I gathered
I generated
I identified
I implemented
I improved
I initiated
I increased
I influenced
I instigated
I integrated
I introduced
I launched
I led
I liaised
I managed
I minimised
I monitored
I motivated
I negotiated
I offered
I organised
I perfected
I performed
I persevered
I persuaded
I planned
I pre-empted
I prepared
I prioritized
I produced
I progressed
I promoted
I proposed
I queried
I quantified
I raised
I recovered
I redesigned
I reorganised
I rescheduled
I resolved
I restored
I saved
I secured
I simplified
I solved
I streamlined
I strengthened
I suggested
I trained
I transformed
I volunteered

Competency 1 Seeing the big picture

"Having an indepth understanding and knowledge and understanding of how your role fits with and supports the organisation's objectives, the wider public's needs and the national interests.

Focusing your activities on those which will meet civil service goals and deliver the greatest value"

Seeing the big picture. No, this is not about going to the cinema to see the latest blockbuster movie nor to the art-gallery to see a van Gogh. It means having an appreciation of how your job fits into the grand scheme of things , how your job is one cog in an interlinked system of cogs in a large machine and that each depends on the other functioning well in order to run to maximum capacity.

Essentially, it has three components : awareness of your organisation, external awareness and vision.

Organisational awareness means that you know your organisation's mission and functions and how its social, political and technological systems operate. This doesn't have to be a detailed knowledge, just a general awareness. It includes its programs, policies, procedures, rules and regulations. You know your company's financial status, whether it is listed on the stock market, its aims, its balance sheet, its leaders, its current budgetary aims.

External awareness means you understand and anticipate how economic, political and social events and trends affect your organisation. These could include budget statements (national and local), strikes, emergencies (terrorism, flooding), Brexit, external competition, new legislation, new technology. External awareness also includes the promotion of partnerships and good working relationships with other organisations, with an understanding of their aims and objectives in order to work across boundaries on solutions and learn best practices.

Vision means that you understand where your organisation is heading and you seek ways and opportunities to make a bigger contribution. You look over the horizon.

In the examples you give, if you have not previously worked in a large organisation, you must tell how you showed an interest in areas of work that were not your own. You must say how you wanted to understand the background and context to how your job fitted into everything and how that then helped you in some way in your own work and perhaps also benefitted the organisation.

Seeing the Big Picture competencies

- I knew my organisation's mission, functions, values , aims and ethos
- I kept myself up to date with my organisation's financial status and budgetary aims
- I read our industry publications
- I discussed with colleagues about how economic, political and social events or trends might impact on our work and tried to predict outcomes
- I made myself aware of my role in the organisation's business continuity plan (for times of sudden emergencies)
- I made efforts to appreciate the background, skills, talents and preferences of all those I worked with, both internally and externally
- I forged good working relationships with external partners and stakeholders
- I spent time talking with suppliers, contractors, customers , programmers and other partners to better understand their job, to see their point of view and to appreciate any difficulties they had in fulfilling our contract.
- I kept myself current with new legislation which might affect my role or our business
- I asked for job rotation to better understand my position in the overall scheme, to learn best practices and to improve inter-departmental relationships
- I asked for a secondment to a different office/ area to develop myself and to see the bigger picture of our organisation's work
- I asked for a term of job-shadowing

Example 1

I had a job in a burger bar. One day, when shopping in a well-known supermarket, I saw that the number of tills had been reduced overnight from 12 to only 4, with 8 new self-service tills now in their place, monitored by just one assistant. I overheard the latter telling a customer that staff had been offered jobs elsewhere but a long distance away.

My colleagues and I would sometimes talk about automation and 'how the robots are coming to take our jobs'. We used to laugh, knowing of course, that jobs in burger-bars would never be done by robots.

A few weeks later, I was again surprised, when I saw the same thing at my local pound shop. I thought to myself that automation was certainly accelerating but thought no more of it.

One weekend, feeling that I wanted a career rather than a job, I went onto our company website to read about management training opportunities. I was astounded to see that our company had not only trialled self-service burger ordering screens but had begun installing them in their U.S stores. For me , the writing was on the wall. It was inevitable that our shop would suffer the same fate.

I looked for a different job in a different sector altogether, one which I felt was robot-proof. Just 2 months after I left the burger-bar, it was automated and unfortunately, 5 of the staff got, not a Big Mac but a Big Smack.

That was an example of how the worker was seeing the bigger picture. He had an awareness of how NEW TECHNOLOGY could impact on his job and he wisely got another job before he lost his.

In your Experiences Autobiography, look for examples of times when you have shown a similar awareness of new technology and acted accordingly. Or the actions of OTHER DEPARTMENTS . Or STRIKES. When writing your answer, be sure to state that it was YOU , who was aware and conscious of the potential impact.

Here now is an example of how it is vital to see the bigger picture by being aware of how external forces such as COMPETITION can impact upon your job, either positively or adversely.

Example 2

I worked in a tea and cake shop in a village. One day, I overheard some of my customers discussing a new planning application that had been submitted to the council. It was for another tea shop.

I realised that if the council granted that application, it might affect our shop adversely. Ours was not the only teashop shop in the village, there was another but I saw the implication and consequence that having a third would be too much competition and that I could end up losing my livelihood.

I told your manager, the owner and I suggested that I could investigate it further later after work. She agreed and so after work, I went along to the council and asked to see the latest applications. Sure enough, there was one for a similar shop.

I photocopied the details and gave them to your manager, who quickly began to assess the possible impact. Even a supermarket not too far away had its own inhouse café now and any threat at all to our consumer base could be fatal. She saw the obvious danger and then began a campaign to oppose the application on the grounds of saturation.

Our loyal customers rallied around us and we managed to have the planning application rejected.

By seeing the bigger picture, that is, by keeping aware of what others are doing outside my own job which might have affected it in some way, I saved my job.

Maybe you only had a Saturday job there but the principle is the same.

In the next examples, we read how it is important to be conscious of how even PHYSICAL FORCES can impinge upon our lives.........

Example 3

I was watching the TV one day and was alarmed at the number of floodings occurring in Britain, some not too far away from me. I was even more alarmed at hearing of the number of people who had not been insured and who had been financially ruined.

I spoke about this to my wife. I decided to investigate further and to my horror, I discovered that our home was on a floodplain and although had never suffered flooding, it might in the future, due to global warming and that the premiums would rise anyway.

I discussed various options as to your course of action. Both of us worked fairly locally in specialised jobs that were difficult to find. We had young kids who were settled in their schools and teenagers who would be approaching exams soon. Moving away from the village would cause massive disruption to our lives and critical job security.

After further discussion and a suggestion from one of our bright kids, a satisfactory solution was found, which was that we sold your present home and moved a short distance away but to much higher ground.

My forethought paid off because the next year, our old home was flooded up to three feet.

My ability to see the big picture - by being aware of circumstances external to my own everyday life - had saved me and my family a great deal of time, stress and money.

Example 4

I lived at one end of a very long avenue and I bumped into a friend, who lived at the other end. During our chat, I mentally took note, when he casually mentioned that a couple of his neighbours had spoken to him of the dry rot in their homes.

When I got home, I researched dry rot, knowing that all the homes in our avenue were more or less similar and were built at the same time. Finding that the cause was primarily due to moisture and a fungus eating the wooden joints, I decided to have a dry rot survey undertaken by a professional.

Although the report concluded that my home did not have dry rot, I was mindful of the reservoir that had been constructed nearby about ten years ago and which I felt had certainly produced more moisture into our local environment. I decided to sell up.

I sold my house and moved away. Five years later, I read in the local paper that the residents of my former avenue had just failed in a tort action against the local council for building a reservoir, which they claimed had led to every one of them contracting dry rot and the value of their homes plummeting.

By seeing the bigger picture, I had saved myself a considerable sum of money.

It is really good ,when writing your examples, you could write about times when you have been awake to how changes might affect your relationships with others, particularly customers. If you have examples of when you foresaw difficulties or threats or opportunities which involved you and partners, customers, contractors, stakeholders, agencies, whatever and tell how you acted upon your awareness for the betterment of yourself or your organisation.

It is also really good if if you have an example which is work-related and which also shows your employer having benefitted because of it........ >>

Example 5

I worked for a large organisation and always kept myself informed as to what was going on in other departments. I could do this because I had friends from all departments and we would meet for lunch each day in the canteen to stay in the loop.

One day, one of them in Payroll told me she had heard that her department would be restructured in three months time, resulting in three new jobs.

I liked the staff there, their higher standards, their culture and most importantly, I had often fancied doing that type of job. I had the intelligence and desire to do it but lacked the necessary qualification and experience.

I set out to find out the requisite qualification (Sage Payroll) and how to get it. To my surprise, it could be gained via a self-paced online course within 2 months. Over the next two months, I did the course at evenings and weekends and gained the qualification.

When the vacancy arose, I applied and overcame their hesitation about my lack of experience by saying that my new training ensured I was at the cutting edge and by saying that the President of the US, the Prime Minister and the Pope all lacked prior experience of their curent roles. I was awarded the job and not only was I happier in it but I was able to bring my knowledge and best practices from my old department to my new one. God helps those who are on the grapevine.

Thanks to your seeing the big picture , your broad thinking, your taking an interest in things other than your own job and networking (socialising) ,, the employer got a multi-functional, multi-skilled worker, whom it could switch between departments in times of necessity, a versatility and flexilbility that employers always find appealing.

Competency 2 Changing and Improving

"People who are effective in this area take initiative , are innovative and seek out opportunities to create effective change.

It is about learning from what has worked well and what hasn't; being open to change and improvement; working 'smarter', in more focused ways.

For leaders. It's creating a culture of innovation; seeking out ways to improve policy implementation and building a leaner, more flexible civil service; making use of alternative delivery models including digital and shared service approaches."

The Adapting to Change Competencies

The interviewer wants to know how you have coped with sudden change . You must demonstrate that had a positive attitude towards it and that you adapted to new working methods. You must show that you see change as a great OPPORTUNITY - to learn new skills and new good working practices, make new friends, improve your CV, and to grow as a person - and not something to be feared. You must show that you were enthusiastic about the change and EMBRACED it rather than feared it. You must show how it benefitted you and the organisation in some way. You must show that you don't collapse or freak out in times of uncertainty or ambiguity.

None of us like constant change . We find it disruptive and I have yet to meet a colleague who likes the capitalist American nonsense of hot-desking (having no desk of your own but having to run round and find an empty one and log into a PC) or multi-tasking (having to do four or five jobs simultaneously) but in your example, you must appear to be flexible and enthusiastic about new ideas.

- I took a positive " I can do it " approach d. to change, seeing it as opportunity to learn skills. I embraced and managed the change.
- I was flexible, enthusiastic and open to change and new ideas
- I was willing to adapt to develop new skills
- I supported and made full use of new technology
- I kept myself up-to-date with new technology and sought to exploit it

- I kept calm, didn't panic in changing circumstances
- I adapted my routine when there was sudden change
- I adjusted positively to rapidly changing priorities and simultaneous demands.
- I adapted my behaviour to new working practices
- I learned from my experiences and those of others and I adjusted my behaviour accordingly
- I changed my behaviour as a result of feedback
- I multi-tasked, playing several different roles
- I revised my plans, decisions and methods in the light of new information
- I was flexible when faced with unexpected obstacles and delays
- I worked effectively in situations of ambiguity and uncertainty

Adapting to Change Examples :

Here are some examples. You should have similar ones in your Experiences Autobiography. In an interview, ensure you include the competencies stated .

Example 1 - You adapted to a new boss or teacher or colleague.
Example 2 - You transferred to a new site or shop or location.
Example 3 - You were asked to take on new tasks and responsibilities. You took them on with enthusiasm.
Example 4 - You learned new software or technology or equipment.
Example 5 - You retrained or went on a course.
Example 6 - You had your shift pattern suddenly altered.
Example 7 - You were suddenly caught up in an unexpected fire, disturbance or crisis. You coped with calmness and positivity.
Example 8 - You lost your job but you adapted -retarining or get two part-time ones
Example 9 - You had to go part-time or job-share. You found another part-time job.
Example 10 - You had to move home and settle into a new environment
Example 11 - You adapted to a changing situation
Example 12 - You reacted appropriately to an unexpected situation
Example 13 - You raised kids. That certainly involved adapting to sudden changes
Example 14 - You volunteered to change shifts or holidays to help someone out
Example 15 - You adapted to new technology at home - a new type of phone/computer/ modem or to a new software system at work
Example 16 - You planned a church fete. That day, there were rain and gales forecast, so rather than cancelling it, you improvised and moved it into the church hall.

Example 17 - You planned you child's birthday party in the garden but when the weather suddenly turned bad, you adapted by moving it indoors.
Example 18 - You were doing one job and were suddenly asked to do another job. So, you delegated some of your work or asked a colleague to take some of your tasks in return for a future favour.
Example 19 - Two staff suddenly left in one week. You readjusted your shifts and also volunteered to do extra hours until a new worker started. Emphasise that you worked smarter as well as simply doing extra hours.

Example 20 - You worked in the storeroom of a shoe shop and were told that in two weeks' time, you would have to work on the till. You adopted a positive approach and asked if you could spend 10 minutes of your lunch observing the till cashiers at work, since you knew nothing about debit cards, etc. That was agreed. When you began your till training, it was SO much easier.

Example 21 :

" When I worked as a secretary, I had arranged the monthly meeting at the office for the managers in our area. That morning when I arrived in work, we found that there was rain coming in through the roof of the conference room. This was only about three hours before the meeting was due to start.

So, I adopted a positive approach and stayed calm. I checked to see if any other rooms could possibly be used but none could. I then quickly phoned each manager's secretary and told them not to let their manager set off until I had found a new location.

Since my manager was off, I took the initiative. I adjusted to the rapidly changing situation by researching local hotels and chose one which was highly recommended by a variety of sources for its high standards of service. I phoned it and booked a room there. I also booked some refreshments. I took the opportunity to have them send details of their services. I then contacted the secretaries again with the precise details of the new location and arranged for the meeting to begin a little later in order to allow everyone sufficient time to arrive.

The result was that the meeting went ahead successfully. Since midweek rates were very cheap and he could network, the regional manager was very impressed and decided to hold all future meetings there. "

Notice how she included some competency indicators of Adapting to Change : *adopted a positive approach.... stayed calm..... adjusted to the rapidly changing situation ....took the opportunity.....*

Example 22 :

In the council's Transport department, I sold tickets to the public and answered enquiries. One Thursday, my Team Leader told me that on Monday, I would be needed in the Information Unit. It was a call-centre environment, containing a large switchboard and a lot of I.T I was unfamiliar with.

So, I embraced the change and adopted a positive approach, seeing it as an opportunity to acquire more skills and efficient working practices. I asked my Team Leader if I could spend some time the next day at the Information Unit, familiarising myself with the equipment and acquainting myself with the staff and layout. She agreed and I spent the Friday there, learning as much as I could.

I liaised with many external partners such as the Police, Coastguard, Emergency Services, the Press, the utility companies etc. I familiarised myself with the tech and even the canteen, toilets and my own route there, so as minimize the strangeness the following week.

The result was that on the Monday, I hit the ground running. Those two weeks were pressurised but because I had planned the change and managed it, it had been a disruption to me but not an upheaval. I had learned new switchboard skills too , which I added to my CV. The Team Leader of the Information Unit was so impressed that he asked me to join his team permanently. I had decided to be the manager of the change, not its victim ."

.

Competency 3 Making effective decisions

" Using sound judgement, evidence and knowledge to arrive at accurate, expert and professional decisions and advice.

Being careful and thoughtful about the use and protection of government information, to ensure its security.

For leaders, it's about reaching evidence-based strategies, evaluating options, impacts, risks and solutions; managing return, while minimising risk; balancing a range of considerations to provide sustainable outcomes".

This competency involves showing the employer that you followed an excellent decision-making model to go forward, rather than making your mind up impulsively, randomly or lazily. You need to show that your decisions are based on EVIDENCE and logical method rather than guesswork or intuition and they are based on DATA rather than assumptions. Stating that your decision-making model involves tossing a coin won't do !

You need to show that you identified your objective, gathered relevant information, evaluated it, generated viable options, critically evaluated the pros, cons and risks and only then made a good decision, which you were ready to modify. I repeat : you must show that you based your decision on data / evidence, not emotion, prejudice or assumption.

We always make better decision in lfe when we are better informed. In your example, you must show that you were well-informed – you gathered lots of info and ensured it was relevant, current, impartial , credible and complete. It must be from reputable, verifiable sources.

You must show that you critically appraised and analysed it by comparing like for like. (i) You can't compare apples with pears (ii) you must be aware of your own conscious and unconscious biases (iii) you must be aware of how stats can be distorted to deceive.

You must filter to get a shortlist of options and consider the potential consequences of each before reaching your final decision. Your example must show your decision was objective and arrived at through reason, not emotion or bias.

In terms of competencies, the interviewer is ensuring you can make well-informed and timely decisions, and that you perceive the impact, implications and potential consequences of decisions you may make.

- I identified my specific objective =what decision had to be made and why
- I collected as much info as possible, from a wide variety of sources
- I ensured the data was current and sources were reputable
- I sorted the relevant from the irrelevant, important from non-important
- I organised the material in a way that aided analysis , like for like, and extracted it appropriately
- I identified and investigated gaps, inconsistencies and ambiguities
- I critically appraised the evidence
- I generated realistic options and discarded unrealistic ones
- I filtered the options into a shortlist
- I assessed the pros, cons, risks and potential consequences of each remaining option
- I confirmed my understanding
- I knew my limitations and involved others with relevant expertise, if necessary
- I made my objective and impartial decision based on the evidence, not emotion, assumption, gossip, hearsay, rumour, guesswork, bias, advertising or incomplete data
- After implementation, I evaluated my decision and confirmed/revised it, taking corrective action based on feedback
- I introduced quality assurance checks, where appropriate.

21 Decision Making Examples

1. You decided to buy any expensive item, such as a house or car or TV.
2. You had to decide whether to buy or rent a home.
3. You decided which school to send your children to.
4. You had to decide which hospital to go to.
5. You had to decide which insurance plan / policy to take out or renew.
6. You had to decide between several job offers.
7. You had to decided between several financial investments / savings.
8. You decided which contractor to hire for a job in your home.
9. You had to make a decision over which university/course to attend.
10. You had to decide whether to emigrate or not.
11. You had to decide to relocate or not.
12. You had to decide between various offers, such as bank loans.
13. You had to decide between a number of job offers
14. You decided to switch bank accounts.
15. You decided to buy-to-let
16. You decided to opt for part-rent, part-mortgage.
17. You decided to change broadband, mobile phone or utility supplier.
18. You decided on a pension scheme

"Give me an example of when you have had to make a major decision."
Example 19 :

A while back, although I had access to a computer at work, I realised that I needed a computer at home . I wasn't sure whether to buy a PC or a laptop. It was a major expenditure and since I couldn't afford to make a mistake, I so had to ensure that I made the right decision.
The first thing I did was I identified my specific objective (buy a computer) and my specific needs - immediate, medium and long term. I asked myself how I would use it mostly. - writing ? music ? family webchats ? How much speed and storage would I need and how soon would it be obsolete. I then collected as much relevant information as I needed from a wide variety of sources, ensuring the info was up-to-date (brochures in shops, websites, chatrooms, consumer groups, independent reviews). I then consulted with computer-shop assistants, friends and work colleagues for advice.

After organising the material in a way that would help analysis and extracting the relevant info appropriately, I generated realistic options for my budget, which led me to decide on a laptop. I filtered the options to a shortlist of three (based on spec, length of guarantee, IT support and price). After assessing the pros and cons and risks of each and confirming my understanding (by emailing the companies), I then made my well-informed and objective decision.

The outcome was that I bought a laptop which served my needs perfectly. I never regretted my decision once and later saw that model go on to win many awards.

Notice he included the competency indicators of Decision Making and these must always be stated in the correct order ...I .identified my specific objective and needs.....I collected as much relevant information as needed ...from a wide variety of sources..... ensuring it was up-to-date....I consulted for advice ..... I organised the material in a way that would help analysis and extracted it appropriately....I generated realistic options.....I filtered the options to a shortlist...I assessed the pros and cons and risks of each option I confirmed my understanding. I made my decision. (This decision-making model should be used for any decision you have made. In your example, you may need to add that you evaluated and then later re-evaluated your decision as you worked, but it wasn't appropriate here.)

- Example 20.......You received some money in a will and wanted to invest it. You researched all the bank & building society accounts, online and off and other options such as Premium Bonds, Fixed Rate Bonds, etc. You evaluated the pros, cons and risks of all of them.

Above all, be sure to say your decision was based on EVIDENCE , whose data was reliable, broad and current and that you carefully evaluated the PROS, CONS, RISKS and POTENTIAL CONSEQUENCES of your decision.

Example 21 :

My phone and broadband (BT)was costing me a fortune (£50/month), so I had to investigate the viability of switching provider to get a better deal.

I identified my needs, budget and the criteria I would use to decide. (Cost per month; any set-up costs; length of contract; customer service standard; leaving cost of current provider; broadband speed). I collected info from a wide variety of sources, ensuring it was reputable, current, complete and with no gaps or irregularities)

Having weeded out the unimportant and organised it to aid analysis, I critically appraised the info (stats deceive and biased adverts exaggerate) and I compared like with like.

I read independent reviews (Which, TrustPilot, TrustedReviews) and the reviews of industry experts (specialist I.T. magazines)

I consulted with others – asked friends, neighbours, shop-assistants and I cleared up any unresolved questions or contradictions – by emailing

I filtered the options down to a shortlist of 3 and then I made my objective & impartial decision by weighing up the pros, cons and risks of each and by thinking through the implications of each option. I kept the '14 cooling-off' details handy, if I wanted to change my mind.

The result was that my objective decision was made on evidence, not emotion or unreliable sources or biased stats or advertising or rumour or hearsay. I switched to TakTalk, with very little disruption and saved £25 per month with no problems whatsover since.

Competency 4 Leading and communicating

"Showing pride and passion for public service. Communicating purpose and direction with clarity, integrity and enthusiasm; championing difference and external experience; supporting principles of fairness of opportunity for all.

For leaders, being visible, establishing a strong direction and a persuasive vision; engaging in a straightforward, truthful way"

From the above, you will see that the Civil Service is combining the leadership competencies with the communication competencies and then the Equality / Diversity competencies

In recent months, depending on the application, candidates have been asked for an example of just one of three, sometimes two, sometimes all three . Bizarrely and unfairly, you are expected to do all that in just 250 words.

My advice is to very carefully read what you are being asked to do here. It is possible but much more difficult to give an example of how you have demonstrated all three in just 250 words. My advice would be to give a strong example which concentrates on just one competency but which incorporates elements and indicators of another. I have listed all three competencies below.

The Leadership Competencies

The interviewer is looking for evidence that you have led and inspired others by your professionalism, integrity, courage, enthusiasm, fairness, inclusiveness and insistence on quality.

- I accepted responsibility when no one else would
- I took decisive action
- I courageously stepped up to the mark in time of need
- I was a role model by my behaviour : always calm, polite, honest, respectful at all times
- I gained trust from others by being trustworthy, keeping promises
- I maintained strict confidentiality at all times

- I encouraged diversity and used its strengths
- I delegated carefully and appropriately
- I resolved conflicts among colleagues and customers
- I fostered teamwork by encouraging and rewarding cooperation
- I inspired and motivated colleagues by coaching / mentoring them towards their self-development goals
- I led with enthusiasm and personal example, mucking in myself
- I gave myself sufficient technical competence to know what to expect from others
- I was alert to potential risks and problems, either in safety or reputation terms
- I delivered, demanded and assisted colleagues to deliver high quality output / service at all times
- I continually sought to improve myself and the team
- I employed the individual talents of each member to best effect
- I continually sought to cut waste
- I rotated jobs to broaden the experience and development of individuals
- I provided good training
- I valued people (by praising them, being approachable and fair, appreciating their efforts, encouraging and guiding their career)
- I communicated the team's objectives clearly and explained my decisions honestly
- I insisted on quality and improvement all the time
- I got people to achieve more than they thought they could
- I led rather than managed (- leaders make things happen and inspire , whereas managers just administer)

Leadership Examples :

Leadership. Give an example of when you have demonstrated this competency.

Example 1 :

One Monday at the HMRC, our call-centre Team Leader was off sick and no rota or duties had been allocated. Our manager was away at a conference that week. Some staff sat around doing nothing, calls were being missed, things were not good.

I showed leadership by suggesting that we have a short meeting. I asked for two volunteers to man the phones. I reminded everyone that our salary and bonuses were linked to our team targets and that we owed a first class service to the customers anyway. I asked for ideas about the rotas and duties, ensuring everyone got to have a say, including the part-timers, interns and school placement kids.

I maintained team morale with positivity and humour.

There were disputes around who wanted to do what and accusations of cherry-picking. I suggested that we worked to our strengths as much as possible : those who preferred taking the short, easy calls to do that and to transfer complex enquiries on to those who preferred the more complex cases or the paperwork cases. I ensured we took into account the early-leaving mothers. My suggestions were adopted.

The outcome was that we met our customer-service targets that week . The customers were happy and we got through it.

I had taken responsibility and by employing the individual skills of each person, fostering inclusion and accounting for the individual diverse needs of people, I had led the team to a peaceful, successful week.

In that example, can you see how I not only showed my leadership skills but I also incorporated indicators of the equality and diversity competency (e.g – I ensured everyone had a say...... I suggested we worked to our individual strengths and preferences....... I took into account the school-runners).

Example 2 : After hearing a colleague maligning our company to a customer, I emphasised the importance of company reputation and got to the bottom of the colleague's discontent. I saved our company's reputation from further harm.

Example 3 : There was an ongoing conflict within our team , which was having an insidious and demoralising effect on everyone. The Team Leader knew about it but seemed unwilling or unable to resolve it and let it drift. I quietly stepped in and resolved it by finding common ground objectives.

Example 4 : When the Area Manager confided in me about his concerns and pleaded with me to be frank, I expressed my frustration that my reported concerns about the lack of quality control on our section were not being addressed. He said that he had been unhappy about our manager for a long time and was unaware about that and he made the necessary changes, thanking me for my courage and insistence on high standards.

The Communication Competencies

The interviewer wants to be sure that you understood that communication is a two-way process ; the need for rapport; that you understood the importance of active listening; you understood the need to check mutual understanding; the need to speak in a logical, structured manner; the need to adapt your communication to suit the listener.

- I actively listened, giving my undivided attention - not interrupting, pre-judging, stereotyping, assuming or preparing my reply
- I established rapport and personalised the encounter, using their name, not account number
- I asked open and probing questions to gain info and understand needs and issues
- I explained why information was required
- I explained complex processes in a simple manner
- I used clear, concise, unambiguous language, avoiding jargon, slang or abbreviations
- I presented information in a structured, logical format and in context
- I pitched my language, content and style at the appropriate level for the listener
- I was positive and polite at all times
- I paused to allow him to contribute
- I checked my understanding
- I checked and confirmed his understanding via questioning
- I summarised my points to ensure clarity and mutual understanding
- I kept focused on the issue in question
- I gave praise, thanks and constructive feedback

- I conveyed disappointing news with tact and sensitivity
- I shared ideas, information and feedback
- I relayed relevant info only to those needing to know it
- I provided knowledgeable and credible responses to queries

The written communication competencies

If the job involves responding by letter or email to enquiries, these may prove useful . Use the main communication competencies above, plus :

- I used a variety of illustrations (charts, graphs) to explain my points, if appropriate
- I used correct grammar, punctuation and spelling
- I organised my ideas clearly
- I wrote in a brief, clear, logical and well-structured manner using appropriate style
- I provided examples and comparisons , if appropriate
- I checked emails / letters / reports had been received and understood
- I chose the right method of communication (email / letter / text / etc to address the recipient

The face-to-face communication competencies

If the job involves considerable face-to-face interaction with customers and visitors, then use the main communication competencies in your answer plus :

- I watched for non-verbal clues such as body language and responded appropriately
- I responded with non-verbal actions (nods and smiles) to show my understanding
- I used a variety of media and graphic aids to reinforce my points and maintain interest
- I was conscious of cultural differences, such as personal space, touching and different body language messages

You might also wish to read the Customer Service competencies and examples in my other book, since there is a great overlap.

The phone communication competencies

All the above plus :

- I was prepared with pen, paper, PC switched on, programs open
- I had all my necessary information at hand
- I was not eating, drinking or chewing
- I answered promptly, within two rings
- I answered with a smile, enthusiasm and warmth
- I gave a greeting and identified myself
- I did not speak too quickly
- I considered time differences of the caller
- I considered possible disabilities of the caller
- I actively listened
- I individualised the call, using the caller's name
- I empathised, if appropriate
- I apologised, if appropriate
- I used appropriate questions - open, closed or probing
- I had the caller spell out any unusual names
- I checked the message I had taken
- If transferring, I first ensured the contact was available
- If transferring, I explained the reason to the caller and gave the contact's name
- If putting on hold, I asked caller's permission first
- I checked my understanding by short paraphrasing
- I followed up on any actions I had earlier promised to the caller

Examples of the Communication Competencies

Example 1

At the Careers Office, I had to give a talk to neighbouring college about our services. I prepared by investigating my target audience by phoning the college tutor to find the make-up of the class : their age-group, background, course and aspirations and what they sought from this talk.

I then considered my style of communication (simple but not condescending) , my content and my presentation (whether to use PowerPoint, video, flipcharts, etc.). Finding the class to be 20 students, I suggested a short video followed by a 10-15 minute talk by me, aided by using flipcharts, followed by a Q&A session. She agreed.

I explained to the class what we would do. While speaking, I used vocabulary which was appropriate to that age and client group. I avoided using jargon, abbreviations or slang. To maintain interest, I used various techniques : I used humour; I paced my speech with pauses, knowing that people have different attention spans; and I alternated my speech with the images on the flowcharts. To help them remember what I said, I used repetition, linking, reinforcement and summarization. After handing out leaflets, I held a Question and Answer session.

The result of the talk was that the Q & A session was very lively and spontaneous, with the students wanting to know much more about our services. The other result was that the college tutor was so impressed that she arranged for the careers visits to become a regular feature at the college.

Notice how some of the indicators of the competency were included in the answer..... investigated the target audience and its needs.... considered my style, content and presentation .....explained in advance what would happen .... avoided jargon, abbreviations and slang... paced my speech with pauses ...alternated my speech with images.......to aid memory, I used repetition, linking, reinforcement and summarization.......I checked understanding..

Example 2

I had a Saturday job in a camera shop and quite often, we had customers in who just wanted a basic model but did not know how to operate it. Since I could complex things in a simple way, my colleagues would refer those customers to me for instructions, once they had paid for their cameras.

Firstly, I established rapport , by saying hello and giving my name and then put them at ease by telling them that digital cameras were much easier to use now than before. When explaining, I used clear, concise and unambiguous language, pitching it appropriately for the listener and I avoided any technical jargon or slang.

After finding out their intended use, I explained how to navigate the different buttons, controls and menu system in a gentle, logical and structured way , taking into account their attention spans. I checked their understanding by asking questions and also by watching for non-verbal clues such as puzzlement . I summarized my points and helped them to remember things by repetition, linking and summarization. I then invited them to try the controls themselves, if they wished to do so.

The result was that the customers said time and again that I had made the whole process so easy and quick to understand. My colleagues and Team Leader were very happy because they could get on with selling more.

In the example above, notice how the following indicators of communication are included.........

I explained complex things in a simple way...... established rapport.....used concise, unambiguous language...... pitched it appropriately...... avoided any jargon or slang .... explained in a logical &structured way..... took into account attention spans..... checked their understanding with questions and by looking for non-verbal clues........summarized my points.

Competency 5 Collaborating and Partnering

> *" Being a team player; working collaboratively and sharing information appropriately; building supportive, trusting and professional relationships with colleagues and a wide range of people inside and outside the civil service.*
>
> *For leaders, being approachable; delivering business objectives through creating an inclusive environment; welcoming challenge, however uncomfortable".*

Collaborating and partnering is the Civil Service's awkward way of saying 'Teamwork' In this competency, you will need to demonstrate how you have worked well with your internal work colleagues and preferably be able to show that you worked well with external colleagues to improve your performance and to further the business.

The interviewer is trying to determine the ways in which you have contributed to the success of a team or to see whether you behave selfishly.

The Collaborating / Partnering/ Teamworking Competencies

- I was friendly, helpful and approachable
- I valued the diverse perspectives, skills, experience, talents and needs of my colleagues
- I shared my ideas and relevant knowledge
- I took trouble to get to know my colleagues , their viewpoints and preferences
- I placed the common group goal above my own goals
- I co-operated with customers, internal and external team members, stake-holders
- I proactively pulled my weight in the team. I mucked in.
- I supported my colleagues with their workload, when I could
- I praised my colleagues when they were successful
- I sought opportunities for cross-functional working and collaboration
- I was flexible over shifts, duties and holidays
- I learned the role of others in the team(s), so as to work better together
- I accepted responsibility for my work
- I employed the diversity and experience of my colleagues to assist me
- I actively participated in team meetings and post-mortems
- I accepted feedback from colleagues on how I impacted on others
- I was always willing to compromise

- I treated all my colleagues with respect and sensitivity at all times
- I was patient, tolerant and didn't play the blame game or gossip
- I maintained team morale with positivity, enthusiasm and humour
- I offered only gentle and constructive feedback
- I balanced my own needs with those of the team
- I formed good working relationships with people both inside my organisation and outside it
- I made myself available by not hiding my email address or extension number
- I knew that T.E.A.M.. means Together Everyone Achieves More and that "There is no "I" in team"

Give an example of when you have demonstrated this competency.

Example 1 :

A colleague was to return to work on the coming Monday after a long absence. There had been major upgrades to our software and changes around the office. Our Team Leader was still off sick and that our manager would be away on a conference, so I determined to assist my colleague's return to work as best I could.

That day, Friday, I retrieved my notes from the last 6 months and photocopied only the ones I thought to be essential . I then stocked up my colleague's stationery drawer with the current new stationery. I contacted our I.T guru and ensured that her PC had been upgraded and was ready to rock.

When my colleague returned, I warmly and sensitively welcomed her back. I informed her of the changes she would need to know about immediately, without overloading her and briefly walked her through the new interface. I assured her that I would be there for any help she needed and that there was no such thing as a stupid question.

I took my lunch break to coincide with her's and kept a discreet eye on her, helping her in a quiet, unobtrusive way, when I saw her queue of customers building up excessively.

The outcome was that she told my manager that she would never have got through the day without my actions and that she wished everyone was as good a team worker as I was. My manager thanked me, both then and in my appraisal.

Example 2 :

When on jury service, the group was very diverse, ranging in ages from about 20 to about 65, from all socio-economic backgrounds, from various races, colour and religions.

We could not agree upon a unanimous verdict and so were ordered to reconsider. For my part, I respected and valued the diverse views, perspectives and experience of all the other members. Whenever I gave feedback, it was always gentle and positive. Similarly, I respected and accepted the feedback from fellow team-members about my suggestions. I employed the diversity of the group to assist my understanding. I contributed to the team by sharing my knowledge and ideas and I contributed to the team morale with humour and enthusiasm.

Unable to reach a 10 to 2 verdict, were again told to go back until we did. Some tempers were getting frayed. Some people were just wanting to go home and were willing to use a coin. I resolved disputes and conflict among team-members who argued, by finding common ground and stating that contradictory views are sometimes just misunderstandings and misinformation. That helped and we finally reached a 10 to 2 majority verdict, which the judge accepted.

The result was that I facilitated in playing a part in ensuring justice was done as much as possible. I had helped a diverse group to work together as a team. I had gained valuable experience working with such a diverse group, which stood me in good stead, helping me get a better job.

He included **some** competency **indicators of Teamwork** : .... respected and valued diverse views, of others.... gave gentle and positive feedback...praised their good suggestions...employed the diversity of the group's skills ...contributed to the team by shared by knowledge and ideas ..contributed to the team morale with humour and enthusiasm...resolved disputes by finding common ground

Collaborating / Partnering / Teamworking Examples :

- I worked in a team
- I played in a sports team, acted in a play, played in a band
- I worked on a project in school that required teamwork. Perhaps Geography or Science or I.T
- I shared information with others in the team
- I offered to help others in my team, when I had finished my work
- I improved team morale with humour
- I worked with neighbours to clear snow or litter
- I contributed to a team in my church
- I participated in a Parent-Teacher forum
- I worked in a team in my hobby group competing against other towns. Chess team ? Footy team ? Brass band ? Choir ? Amateur Dramatics ?
- I participated in a team when I was sent on a course
- I resolved conflict within my team
- I stayed longer after work to help a colleague
- I did more than my allocation of work
- I served on a jury
- I swapped my day off or holidays to help a team colleague in need
- I typed and printed menus or the minutes at a food bank or a residents association
- I showed flexibility over shifts

Example 3 : One of my new colleagues didn't have much experience in using Outlook and was having difficulty using it and missing meetings, so I offered to help her out for a few hours after work. Since then, she's never had a problem with Calendar. It has not only helped her but also helped the team meet its targets.

Example 4 : You informed your colleague, who had returned to work after a period of illness, of the new changes, procedures and modifications to the software interfaces, rather than see her struggle on her first days back. You prioritized the info, giving her only the most relevant material. She praised you to the Team Leader.

Understand that collaboration is NOT about being in perfect harmony. It is wrong to believe that good teamwork means avoiding disagreement. Good teamwork is synthesising different perspectives and coming up with new solutions as a result, otherwise you will only ever get conformity, dullness, tunnel vision and groupthink.

Far better to have an environment where people can disagree on a professional level , without getting caught up in personal clashes.

Example 5 :

The Council had just outsourced its cleaning and security contracts at the Town Hall to external private companies. Unfortunately, this led to problems with staff non-attendance, poor record-keeping and cleanliness issues. My team leader mentioned his imminent scheduled meeting with the external partners.

I offered to hold the timesheets of both companies at our reception-desk and counter-sign staff in and out. I suggested it would pre-empt disputes over absences and attendance times and was also a way of fostering inter-agency collaboration.

A week later, my Team Leader said he had put forward my proposal and it had been accepted. From then onwards, after consultation with their managers over their preferences, I and my reception colleagues counter-signed all timesheets accurately and fairly.

The results were a win-win situation for all parties. 1- The Town Hall was cleaner and safer, as attendance and time-keeping improved dramatically. 2 The managers of the external partners expressed their delight with the arrangement and with the spirit of cross-organisation partnering. 3-My Team leader praised my suggestion and said the Council Leader was pleased to hear of our frictionless, seamless co-operation between the public and private sectors.

Finally, some cleaners thanked me for a fairer system, saying that they no longer had to do the remedial work of the skivers before starting their own shift.

Competency 6 Building capability for all

> *" Focusing on continuous learning for oneself ; being open to learning; keeping one's knowledge and skillset current and evolving.*
>
> *For leaders, it is giving clear, honest feedback; supporting teams to improve and succeed; creating a learning and knowledge culture".*

Building capability is the Civil Service's strange way of saying 'Continuous self-improvement'. The Japanese have a word for it , ***kaizen,*** which means 'constant change for the better'. In the context of this competency, it means frequently looking at your work and your performance and trying to improve efficiency by constantly improving your knowledge and skills and your processes.

Take notice and be careful. When you write your answer to this competency, do not write how you thought of a good idea, which reduced waste in your office or which made more money or attracted more sales. Here, you are expected to explain **how you improved your skills and knowledge.** It is about self-improvement, not bright ideas. So be sure to stay on topic.

The self-improvement competencies

- I continuously checked that the quality and coverage of my work reached the required standard
- I frequently reviewed my performance to identify weaknesses and training / development needs
- I learned and shared best working practices and tips from colleagues
- I learned from my mistakes and those of others
- I read as much as I could find about my job, so as to benchmark my skills against others in my sector / industry
- I took advantage of all inhouse training , including the company's intranet
- I took online courses including Youtube and the free online university courses to expand my knowledge
- I developed my skillset through evening classes
- I networked with others – at the water-cooler, photocopier,kitchen,lift
- I took part in focus groups

- Joined an online discussion group, such as Yammer
- I requested job rotation to learn other duties and to expand my CV
- I requested to work in another branch for a while to learn more best practices
- I listened to customers, suppliers and contractors to learn their views
- I participated in quality circles to improve both personal and team quality
- I requested an 'acting-up' role to cover temporary Team Leader absence
- I asked for a 'job-shadowing' role to learn the work of a colleague
- I asked for temporary secondment to another branch / department/ abroad to broaden my expertise and experience
- I regularly sought feedback about my work from my Team Leader and colleagues and acted upon it to remedy my weak areas
- I evaluated my progress
- I conducted a training-needs (skills gap) audit and asked my Team Leader for time or resources for me to address these
- I encouraged and supported colleagues in their self-improvement, since that aided the whole team

There are many ways in which you might have improved your knowledge and skills. Here are some short examples to get you thinking.

Example 1 : You all had 100 legal forms to check each day (or 100 widgets to pack into a box per hour.) You noticed that a few of your colleagues were much faster than you at doing it, with no loss of quality. You humbly asked them something along the lines of "Hey, it's fantastic the way you get your work done so quickly . Have you got any tips ? Is there some sort of magic trick involved ?" One or two wouldn't help but two gave invaluable advice, which speeded up your work no end.

Example 2 : You took the initiative to come in early each morning to take full advantage of the company's online training modules to improve your expertise in some Microsoft Office modules , which were relevant to your daily work or helped you to master your inhouse software programs.

Example 3 :

> I worked in a betting shop. I asked my manager to let me 'job-shadow' him for a week, so that if ever he was off sick, I would be able to deputise in his absence . In that way, disruption on our section would be minimised because it would be better than a total outsider coming in.
>
> After getting permission, he agreed and one week, when we were fully staffed and not too busy, he allowed me to sit next to him and listen, watch and do what he did. I ensured that I learned as much as I possibly could, asking many questions and learning by actually doing whenever possible. I also saw my own role in a better light. I took his feedback very seriously.
>
> Six months later, when he went off sick for an operation, I asked the Area Manager if I could stand in, citing my job-shadowing experience. He agreed and I deputised for our manager for two weeks and was told I had done well.
>
> A few months later, a manager in another branch went on maternity leave. I applied for her temporary post and got it, due to the experience I had gained from job-shadowing and deputising. When she decided not to return to work, I was promoted to Branch Manager.
>
> After a year, I asked the Area Manager if I could job shadow him.☺

Example 4 : You bought the two books by Mike New about job competencies to help you benchmark your skills against those of others in your industry

Example 5 : You bought online courses or took free ones to improve your technical knowledge and gain industry qualifications. Although you had prior experience, you lacked the paper qualifications , so you took the relevant courses to update your expertise and also to validate your skills with certification.

Example 6 : You improved your Microsoft Office skills at home without spending a penny by watching Youtube videos and by reading library books.

Example 7 : You asked for a meeting with your Team Leader / Manager to discuss your future. You told them that you did not want to stay on the bottom all your life but had ambitions to move up the ladder. You asked them to list your skills gaps / training needs and to map out your development plan. You agreed to meet weekly or monthly to get feedback, to correct any skills gaps and to identify any competencies you will need for the next rung of the ladder.

Example 8 : You suggested a Training Needs grid sheet be put up on your staff notice board . Any staff member who felt that they needed training or retraining in any area of their job could write that on the sheet. Eg – How to scan; how to print back to back; how to change cartridges; how to use the fire-extinguisher; how to change the water cooler ; etc. Anyone else needing that training could add their name and Team Leader could arrange workshops. Alternatively, a staff survey could be carried out in which the Team Leader listed a whole set of skills and those seeking training just ticked those required.

Example 9 : I got up an hour early every Saturday morning and taught myself to type using an online tutor. It cost me nothing, it took me only 9 weeks to reach a speed of 30 words per minute and got me a job in a solicitor's office. It didn't even wake my baby either as my keyboard is very quiet ! (typeonline.co.uk or typingclub.com)

In the council's Transport department, I sold tickets to the public and answered enquiries. One Thursday, my Team Leader told me that on Monday, I would be needed in the Information Unit. It was a call-centre environment, containing a large switchboard and a lot of I.T I was unfamiliar with.

So, I adopted a positive approach to the change, seeing it as an opportunity to acquire more skills and efficient working practices. I asked my Team Leader if I could spend some time the next day at the Information Unit, familiarising myself with the equipment and acquainting myself with the staff and layout. She agreed and I spent the Friday there, learning as much as I could.

I liaised with many external partners such as the Police, Coastguard, Emergency Services, the Press, the utility companies etc. I familiarised myself with the tech and even the canteen, toilets and my own route there, so as minimize the strangeness the following week.

The result was that on the Monday, I hit the ground running. Those two weeks were pressurised but because I had planned the change and managed it, it had been a disruption to me but not an upheaval. I had learned new switchboard skills too , which I added to my CV. The Team Leader of the Information Unit was so impressed that he asked me to join his team permanently. I had decided to be the manager of the change, not its victim ."

Example 11 :

While I was on my month's induction course at my new job with the Tax Office, I found that MS Outlook would be used extensively and to a sophisticated level, including using Calendar for meetings . Although I had used email before, such as Google , I did not have those skills and I was going to need them every day .

So, I took the initiative and I asked for training in Outlook. This was refused due to lack of resources. I immediately looked for any online training modules on the inhouse intranet system , found some and asked I.T to set me up but was refused on the grounds that I was not to be given full access until my induction was complete. I would be under enough pressure dealing with the public, handling new software, new systems in a new job ,having targets without having to stumble through an email system .I wanted to deliver a speedy, high-class service.

I took the initiative again by buying a Teach Yourself Outlook manual and learning the course at the library. I also updated my Windows knowledge and other MS programs skills to deliver the best performance possible. I then had my training assessed and certified. (My friends said I should be certified. ☺).

The result was that my initiative had meant that I hit the ground running, delivered a first class-service, gained new certificates and even being asked for help by colleagues who had started the same day "

Competencies 7 to 9 and how they differ

A longstanding accusation against the Civil Service is that it is stuffed with people who have come straight from school or university and who have never worked in the private sector and have nor real business instinct . The claim is that many staff have no interest in protecting the public purse or ensuring the public is getting value for money and the many reports of misspending and overspending and sheer waste show the claims to be largely true. Therefore, efforts have finally been made to recruit staff who can appreciate the responsibility of protecting the public finances and show a money mindset at all times. Many people regard these three competencies as very much the same and they have difficulty differentiating between them. They are subtly different.

Simply stated , Competency 7 **'Achieving Commercial Outcomes'**, is about being money-minded while you work. It is about having a business instinct and **spotting opportunities to make or save money.** For this, visualise a LIGHT BULB symbolising a new idea, a new notion of making or saving money.

Competency 8 **'Delivering Value for Money '** is about **ensuring that you get what you have paid for**. It is about revenue protection and contract compliance. For this, visualise BATTLING BESSIE, HOLDING UP A CONTRACT IN COURT. She certainly knows how to stand up for her rights. She even went to night school to learn about contract law.

Competency 9, **'Managing a Quality Service'** means **ensuring quality is maintained at all stages of your work**. It is about promoting the highest standards in everything that is done. For this, visualise a man in his forties in a factory. He is a SUPERVISOR WEARING A WHITE LAB COAT. He is wearing glasses with black frames. He has a clipboard, a stopwatch, and a powerful magnifying glass. He is a very fussy, strict quality control inspector, who won't tolerate shoddy work.

All these three competencies involve the principle of your ' **adding value'** to the employer's business, so you must be sure to state that because that is what they will be looking for in your answers.

Competency 7 Achieving commercial outcomes

" To maintain an economic long-term focus. Have a commercial, financial and sustainable mindset to ensure all activities add value. Work to stimulate economic growth.

For leaders, it is identifying economic, market and customer issues; using those to promote innovative business models and commercial partnerships to deliver greatest value; to ensure tight commercial controls of finances, resources and contracts to meet strategic priorities"

At first, competencies 7 and 8 look very similar : ' Achieving commercial outcomes' and 'Delivering value for money'.

To some extent, they are and there is some overlap but they do differ.

'Achieving commercial outcomes' means thinking in financial terms. It means having a business instinct. It means that you should always have an attitude of examining how you work to seek ways to save your employer money in the long term. Both competencies involve controlling costs but this particular competency means that **you thought of a new initiative to make or save money.**

When giving examples, you will have to narrate how you thought of a new process or how you made an existing process more efficient, either in terms of time saved or money saved. You had a LIGHTBULB moment.

In the last few decades, organisations have adopted the Toyota principles of 'Lean' working, in which all waste is eliminated.

The main areas of waste are :

Unnecessary movement : having to move items/work/people unnecessarily, which can waste time and risk damaging or losing the item and risk harm to staff. Example : Staff having to attend the yearly conference to hear the CEO's report, when it could equally have been delivered by mass email. Example : 3 or 4 local managers travelling to a meeting, when a video conference call could have been set up instead. Example : Human Resourses calling candidates to a first stage interview, when it could have been done via Skype or Google. All these are graphic examples of waste of movement. Example : Staff having to commute to work due, when they could easily work from home, if allowed by their boss.

Other examples of unnecessary movement can be a result of poor ergonomics (design of office layout or furniture). Example : Workers having to waste time walking up 2 flights of stairs to the canteen for their tea break or to the toilet. Example : having frequently used items at a distance (photocopier, printer), resulting in hundreds of wasted hours a year.

Errors : Examples : Errors in poorly written software can lead to waste, forcing staff to carry out remedial procedures; staff can commit costly errors through being inadequately trained or through a lack of attention to detail (talking, daydreaming, multi-tasking). Errors can arise through goods being damaged or procedures not being adhered to, carelessness, all of which require costly rectification.

Duplication of work : Making / doing things twice. Example : Having to re-enter data twice could be as a result of poor concentration or poor training or poor procedures, which fail to trap double-entry.

Over-production / Over-processing : making / doing more than is necessary or before it's needed. Example : having a 6 point checklist, when a 3 point one will achieve the same result. Example : printing out and sending a paper copy of something to a customer , when you have already emailed it to them. Example : issuing a receipt to a customer, who hasn't requested one.

Delay : Having to wait for products or services to be delivered. Example: having to wait for responses from customers / partners. (Put deadlines on them!) Example : Being delayed due to train strikes or road traffic jams/accidents. . Example : Time wasted by having to wait in queues at the photocopier, caused by having insufficient resources.

Incorrect inventory : Being understocked or overstocked. Products or necessary tools being out of stock, causing delays to your work. Example : Overstocked of shelves, using up valuable space and paying rent on floor space needlessly, which could be used to sell other "in demand" products that customers want.

Poor communication : Examples : Staff duplicating work due to poor communication amongst themselves. Example : Public and customers being ill-informed, resulting in errors by them or repeated callbacks and reworks by staff. Example : An absence of or poor communication to customers (such as vague/

ambiguous/ jargon-filled or insufficient information) leading to errors and many callbacks, phone enquiries, complaints, letters for clarification or rectification. Example : A poorly designed form either confuses customers or fails to capture all the requisite information and results in many follow-up calls by staff having to seek clarification or additional information.

Missed opportunities : Example : Staff failing to appreciate the value of customers' complaints. Example : Staff failing to use cutomer feedback as a means to improve and to focus on true needs and demand. Example : Staff failing to recognise patterns in breakdowns and problems, wasting the opportunity to eradicate them.

The above are all examples of waste and examples of which, if you are constantly aware of ways of saving money, you can compare to your own experiences to use quote of times when you have added value by saving money.

Give an example of when you have demonstrated this competency.

14 examples of Achieving Commercial Outcomes

Example 1 :

In my last role, the post was despatched manually. After weighing and franking everything, the staff entered the details into a postbook. Once, when I needed to find something about a Special Delivery postage, I happened to notice that we could do our posting online via the Royal Mail site and save £60 per week.

I took the initiative to read more about it and then to phone them up for more details. I then wrote a short proposal to my manager explaining the situation and outlined how much we would save by using the Royal Mail online service. I explained that as well as being cheaper, it would also be quicker. I also explained that we could easily print off the details and that he could easily analyse posting costs and volumes at any time via our account.

He objected that we would be in a fix if our IT ever went down and were unable to send our mail, which absolutely had to go out that day. When I reassured him that I had already enquired about that scenario and been told that under those circumstances we could revert back to using our book, attaching an explanatory message on the slip, he agreed and told me to set up our account.

The result was that my initiative saved our company over £ 3000 every year and also added value in terms of the many man-hours saved.

Key points to notice :

The C.A.R format was used : Circumstance, Action taken and then the Result.

Most time was taken up describing the action the writer took.

The writer said what HE did and how he overcame objections.

The story had a positive, successful ending for the employer.

The writer quantified the success with figures.

The writer stated that he had added value to the work.

Example 2 : You worked in a chain of chemists, which had 20 stores. You suggested to your boss, the owner of these, that he could make considerable savings if he replaced all the current strip-lighting ceiling panels with the new energy-efficient LED solutions. You convinced him and as a result of that upgrade, you reduced his energy consumption by 1 million kWh per year. The project paid for itself within three years and every subsequent year brought him substantial savings. You were rewarded handsomely.

I suppose you could say that really was an example of a lightbulb moment !

Example 3 : You worked in a very large organisation, which had many departments spread over a large site. It received a great amount of deliveries and mail but there were multiple problems : staff didn't know when their items had been been received, itmes had gone missing, etc. You suggested the company use a new 'track and trace' app, which gave a full audit trail of all accountable mail items. It gave full item audits, signed proof of delivery and courier tracking. Email notifications could be generated to inform customers of the progress and whereabouts of their item. Data from the app gave managers full visibility of spend to streamline operations and business rules could be applied to support SLAs.

Example 4 : You re-organised a filing system , either manual or computerised, which improved efficiency by preventing errors and by saving time and reducing complaints.

Example 5 : You improved productivity when you suggested the introduction of a video-conferencing system to save staff travelling time and travel costs.

Example 6 : You suggested to your boss to stop renting your bins from the council. You had been paying the council both for their rental and their emptying. You persuaded him of the long-term financial benefits of buying your own bins. Once the initial outlay had been paid off, you began to save £600 every year.

Example 7 : You searched for and then downloaded apps, which improved productivity. One app alerted your drivers to roadworks /delays, thus saving time and fuel. Another was a conversion app, which helped you convert measurements faster or more accurately when dealing with your customers, thereby allowing you to make more sales. You worked in logistics and you downloaded an app which showed all local toilets. In that way, your drivers saved valuable time and fuel. Instead of driving around searching for a toilet, they could locate one easily. Not sat-nav but sat-lav .☺

Example 8 :

When I started in my last job, I was horrified to see the baskets underneath the photocopier/printers overflowing with discarded sheets that staff had erroneously or needlessly printed. After walking around and inspecting all the wastepaper baskets beside staff desks, I found a similar picture : forests of paper were being printed off each day needlessly.

Examination of the discarded paper at the main printer showed obvious signs of experimentation at back-to-back printing; printing landscape spreadsheets in portrait mode; the same document printed with various incorrect margins, etc.

At our weekly staff meeting, when asked for suggestions for improvements, I challenged this wastefulness. Firstly, I suggested that a signature be added to the bottom of everyone's email asking them to only print a hard copy if really necessary and only to do so after spellchecking and proofreading . Secondly, I suggested that a bright notice or poster be prominently displayed above the photocopier asking staff to consider the environment before overusing paper. Thirdly, I suggested either having a photocopier/printer guru , who knew how to operate all the functions to whom staff could seek assistance, rather than waste many sheets of paper in experimentation or else having training sessions in all the machine's functions for those requesting them.

My ideas were accepted and implemented. After six months, the usage of paper had dropped by 25 reams per month, thus saving my employer around £600 per year.

Example 9 : You analysed all the forms/ invoices/ sales dockets being used and designed a new form, which incorporated the questioned into one or two sheets , thereby saving paper. The emphasis must be on how you brought something new into being , which resulted in a financial benefit to your employer.

Example 10 : You devised a new Excel spreadsheet to quickly record customer feedback or responses by simply clicking on one of four pre-designed boxes. This led to an adjustment to the discount that was being offered to your customers and subsequently a 20% increase in new customers.

Example 11 : You noticed that a document, which contained a set of particular procedural steps, was often being mislaid by staff and reprinted . So, to reduce waste, you scanned it, uploaded it to the system, placed it on the 'shared drive' and informed everyone of its location. You suggested to them that they could save it to their desktop with a shortcut. From then onwards, productivity was improved because staff were finding it more quickly. Also, no one was reprinting that document , thus saving needless waste.

Example 12 : When a neighbour told you she was selling up and moving abroad for good, you remembered that she had thousands of books. You asked her what she would do with them all. She said that you could have them. After she left, you sold them on ebay. That shows you have commercial instinct.

Example 13 : You shamelessly haggled over the price of something in a shop to reduce its cost. You eventually got the nickname Marvin Hagler from your friends, after your ability to haggle for a lower price. That is commercial instinct.

Example 14 : You worked in a team in a very large shopping mall. There was to be an installation of a new escalator . When you noticed that it was scheduled for a weekend, you wrote a small proposal to your manager stating the potential loss of revenue caused by the disruption at the busiest time (weekend) could be avoided if we insisted to the contractor that the work was done midweek. He agreed and thanked you in your annual appraisal. (When you've seen one, you've seen a mall. ☺)

0-0-0-0

Remember, your example does not have to be work-related : it merely has to demonstrate that you have a money-making mindset, a "business instinct".

If you are not "money-minded" by nature, you have to pretend to be, in order to get the job. In return, the employer will then pretend to care about you.

For more examples, think of ways in which you have acted to save yourself money in the past. Best of all, try to think of ways in which you have acted to improve productivity for yourself or others or to SAVE your employer money in the long term. (Some people have done this by leaving their job .)

In each case, be sure to state how your new idea added value by improving efficiency / productivity or bringing in more revenue or by decreasing costs.

Competency 8 Delivering value for money

"Efficient, effective and economic use of taxpayers' money; seeking out and implementing solutions which achieve a good mix of quality and effectiveness, for the least outlay.

Basing decisions on evidenced info; following agreed processes and policies and challenging these, if they prevent value for money.

For leaders, to embed a culture of value for money and to work collaboratively across boundaries to maximise strategic outcomes".

Delivering Value for Money

Ultimately, the concept of 'value for money' is always determined by the customer. If the customer believes he is not receiving what he has paid for, then he will not return.

Value for money means getting what you have paid for – it means getting what you have paid for in terms of quality, in quantity and in being delivered on time. It is also maintaining that value by reducing waste and usage.

For this competency, you will need to provide an example of how you have ensured that you have received everything you paid for, that it is to the quality standard you agreed and that it was delivered on time. Typically, the Civil Service has misnamed this as 'delivering' value for money, when actually, you are ***ensuring*** value for money.

'Quality' means that it has to be **'fit for purpose'**. If you take delivery of an order from a supplier, it has to be exactly what you ordered in terms of materials, size, quantity, measurements, colour, etc ; it has to be delivered to you without any defects, damage or parts missing; and it has to be delivered to you within your pre-agreed timescale. The same principle applies to services as well as goods. If any of these are not to the pre-agreed contract and you are having to spend any time at all on complaints or re-orders, then you are not getting value for your money.

Remember the symbol – you are battling Bessie IN COURT and you are absolutely determined to get value for your money. You will ensure the other party fulfils the contract in full.

12 examples of Delivering value for money

Example 1 :

I began work at a small bathroom company. I found that the team was spending a lot of time going back to the suppliers because they had delivered the wrong orders, either in terms of colour of tiles or their design or size. This was costing the company a lot of time and manpower in complaints due to delays, to repeat calls and to repeat reception of re-deliveries.

I investigated and found that it was because the order-taker on the supplier's side was too slapdash about recording precisely what was ordered. Our orders were being taken over the phone and he was always assuming he knew exactly what our callers wanted and making guesses. He failed to check 'mutual understanding'.

I requested to meet the supplier and got him to accept email orders from our team. I designed a standard order template From that point onwards, all orders were submitted by email on that template I had designed. I had also got an agreement that all email orders would be acknowledged within 1 hour and that if any problems arose on their side with any of our orders, they were to immediately phone me on my mobile or any of my team colleagues.

The result was that incorrect deliveries were eliminated altogether, thus saving around 30 man hours or £250 per week. I added value by ensuring that our company now got what it had paid for and I set in motion a process to resolve future issues more speedily.

Sometimes, ensuring value for money can mean ensuring compliance or adherence to agreed contracts. You must show that you are not naïve, that you are nobody's fool and that you won't allow others to rip you off, when it comes to getting value for your money, as we shall see in this next example.

Example 2 : **Your answer :**

Our business was having its premises extended. The Project Manager was off ill and I was asked to deputise. I noticed that there was a considerable degree of ' scope creep ', (a series of small, gradual changes to a project or contract, which accumulate significantly to affect it.) The builders were making what they considered to be minor changes and suppliers were substituting alternative, possibly inferior materials to what had been laid down in the contract, without formal approval. Also, I noticed that jobs were taking longer and costing more than originally agreed. Work was being delayed then done on overtime rates.

So, I monitored this ' scope creep ' by ensuring all expenditure, timesheets and unauthorised changes / substitutions of any kind, were carefully recorded. I then prepared weekly reports and submitted them to my supervisor for action. By doing so, I was ensuring that our company was not getting ripped off or being taken advantage of in any way.

Upon the Project Manager's return, thanks to my records and reports, he claimed back the amounts we had been overcharged in subtle, insidious ways, which came to £7,000.

By ensuring the contract was being rigidly adhered to, I ensured our company got full value for its money.

You ensured you got what you had paid for.

Example 3 : You worked for a firm of solicitors. There was a great deal of typing/word-processing that had to be done each day and much of it was outsourced to homeworkers. Most work was returned to a high standard but two workers consistently submitted work which had errors. You called them in and explained the necessity for zero-tolerance of errors in such important work. Although they had used spell-checkers, they were not checking for the incorrect use of their/there/they're, where/were/we're , to /too/two , knew/new, etc. You insisted that they visually proofread everything twice before they submitted their work to you . Their work improved to the required standard so that you were now getting the standard that you were paying for at last.

Example 4 : You began work in a warehouse. You noticed that about 5% of the stored stock had been put aside as 'damaged'. It was assumed that the stock had been damaged in transit within the warehouse but you suspected otherwise. You began to observe the receipt of incoming goods and noticed that they were unloaded by forklift trucks straight from wagons into your loading bays and the delivery notes signed for immediately, without any inspection of the goods being undertaken. You established a new process by which the loading bay staff had to visually check the delivered boxes and bags for shortages or obvious damage and to refuse any that appeared to be damaged. They also had to log all instances of refusals and the reasons and these were examined regularly to reduce them. This cut down stock loss by over £12,000 per year. You ensured that you got what you had paid for in full.

Example 5 : You began a new job in a small builder's office, where invoices were frequently paid late because they were getting mislaid. This was incurring unnecessary late-payment charges and also interest. Your employer was not getting the value for his money because some of his staff were working inefficiently and losing him money.

You devised a system to ensure that all invoices would be actioned in sequence and within 2 working days and that any problems would be flagged up to you . This terminated the late-payment fines, thus saving the company approx £ 500 per year and ensuring the boss was now getting value for money.

0-0-0

Ensuring value for money is not only getting what you have paid for but also maintaining the value of the goods you have paid for by **reducing waste.** It is about having a ' **lean** ' approach to work and your resources.

Ensuring value for money can mean that when your employer has spent a considerable amount of money on something, its value is not degraded by wasting it or abusing it in various ways.

Example 6 : You worked in a company, where the staff were rather complacent about turning off lights and heaters after work. After seeing the energy bills your boss was receiving, you suggested to him that he was not getting value for money because some of the staff were going home leaving lights on, leaving heaters , fans or humidifiers on, leaving computers on, etc. You estimated that his bill would be reduced by 10%, if staff would be mindful of waste and misuse. You introduced a check system , whereby the 'last out' had to sign to state he had checked that all lights and equipment had been turned off. The result was that his energy bills did indeed fall by around 10% and he began to get value for his money.

Example 7 : When your stationery contract came up for renewal, you suggested that it was changed so that the supplier's drivers had to deliver the stationery to your individual stationery hubs on each floor , not just your loading bay. That was agreed , at no extra cost, thereby saving many man hours of staff having to distribute it throughout the building. You ensured that you got more for your money.

Example 8 : When you started a new job, you noticed that the company still used paper towels in the toilets, because they had "always done things that way". You made a business case, via a Powerpoint presentation, for ditching paper towels for an electric hand dryer. You researched materials you had seen online, showing that even if the paper towels had been responsibly sourced, most can't be recycled and still needed costly binbags, maintenance and collection. Hand dryers soon repaid their initial outlay, were far more hygienic and easily cheaper to run in the long term. The manager was convinced by your argument and switched to electric dryers. There were no savings enjoyed in the first two years due to the expenditure on the dryers but the cost benefits started to show through from the third year onwards, when the company saved around £300 per year. The company was now deriving value for its money, when it came to the matter of money it was spending on drying hands. The company had cleaned up its act by washing its hands of an outdated, unhygienic practice.

Example 9 : When a junior manager, staff meetings were unnecessarily long and unproductive. You limited the length of meetings to devote more time to customer service, thereby increasing customer satisfaction and sales. The employer was now getting more value for money for his staff salaries. (*" A meeting is an event where minutes are taken but hours are wasted".)* ☺

Example 10 : When starting as a supervisor, you found that staff were taking ten-minute smoking breaks, five or six times per day, on top of their lunch breaks. You introduced a regime to limit the breaks to five minutes and twice a day, thus ensuring the boss was now getting value for the salaries he was paying out.

Example 11 : Your new gardening contract was up for renewal. Your mower constantly needed expensive repairs. So, you suggested to your Residents' Association that the gardeners use their own mower as part of the new contract, rather than your mower. That was agreed and you saved £120 per year in repair charges, thus ensuring you got value for your gardening contract money.

Example 12 : You replaced your existing phone, broadband or energy provider, saving you £100 per year.

Perhaps you replaced your boyfriend or girlfriend for a better one , which saved you money or stress in the long term. ☺

Competency 9 Managing a quality service

> *" Valuing and modelling professional excellence to deliver objectives, taking into account diverse customer needs and requirements.*
>
> *Planning, organising and managing time and activities to deliver a high-quality, efficient service, using programme, project and risk-management approaches.*
>
> *For leaders, it is creating an environment to deliver operational excellence and creating the most appropriate and cost-effective delivery models."*

'Quality' means **'fit for purpose'.** If you take delivery of an order from a supplier, it has to be exactly what you ordered in terms of materials, size, quantity, measurements, colour, etc ; it has to be delivered to you without any defects, damage or parts missing; and it has to be delivered to you within your pre-agreed timescale. The same principle applies to services as well as goods.

Quality is also about meeting the minimum standard required to satisfy your customers' needs. Shoes must last more than a few months before falling apart. A washing-up liquid can claim to be high-quality if one squirt is sufficient to clean a family's dirty plates after a meal. A poor quality washing-up liquid requires several squirts.

It is important to understand the difference between Quality Control and Quality Assurance.

Quality control is where **finished** products and delivered services are checked by inspectors to see if they meet the set standard. However, this can be a costly process as there can be a high degree of waste and a need for reworks.

Quality assurance is where **quality is built into all stages** of the production process and involves all staff at every stage. Everyone is an inspector. This principle is known as Total Quality Management, (**TQM**). In this way everyone takes responsibility for delivering quality, resulting in zero defect production. Quality assurance includes quality control as its final stage.

For example, in a juice factory, random bottles of orange squash are selected, as they come off the production line and tested for the correct percentage of orange concentrate. If found faulty and further tests on other bottles in the batch reveal similar faults, the whole production run might have to be scrapped and reworked, proving costly in terms of money, man hours and materials. That is quality control.

If the ingredients are monitored in some way at earlier stages in the production - perhaps as they are mixed and then poured into the bottles - then that is quality assurance.

The Quality Assurance Competencies

- I accepted responsibility for the quality of all my work at every stage
- I participated in Quality Circles, to learn and exchange ideas
- I learned efficiency techniques from colleagues and shared my 'best practices', to ensure consistently high standards
- I benchmarked my performance (i.e compared it to the best practices in my industry / field)
- I retrained myself periodically to stay cutting-edge
- I attained quality-control certification (such as ISO 9000)
- I employed a ' Right First Time ' approach in my work
- I adopted a ' Zero Defects' philosophy and was intolerant of sloppy, careless, lazy work by myself and others
- I changed my work after feedback from managers and colleagues
- I ensured service levels were maintained, flagging up risks and concerns
- I kept colleagues , customers and partners informed of plans, problems or delays in our common work
- I identified recurring weaknesses in our processes and either resolved them or escalated them
- I facilitated the easy reporting of complaints and suggestions by our customers, seeing them as a welcome, costless and a valuable source of grassroots feedback
- I acted upon complaints and useful feedback to improve the quality of our processes
- I worked on improving my 'Attention to Detail' competencies – (below)

5 examples of managing a quality service

Example 1 :

When I started at a sweet factory, the returns-rate was very high, customer complaints took up so much of staff time and the customers were taking their business elsewhere, due to errors. The firm was being let down by its weak quality assurance system.

After conducting a thorough investigation, I sent a set of proposals to the owner. I suggested having TQM (Total Quality Management), promoting a culture of quality amongst all employees, so that everyone was made responsible for quality at every stage of the process; the introduction of Quality Circles (monthly groups to discuss quality problems); sharing of 'best practices' amongst all staff, so as to ensure consistently high standards; a liaison with the local Chamber of Commerce to introduce (a) benchmarking (identifying and adopting the best practices of competitors in that industry) plus (b) quality certification such as ISO 9000 or similar and (c) the identification of training needs ; the adoption of a 'Right-First-Time' approach, with a 'Zero-Defects' philosophy, to prevent remakes, thereby saving time and money.

The owner adopted my suggestions in full. Not only was there a 90% reduction in the number of items returned for reworks but the staff felt more engaged and more motivated and began to take more pride in their work, especially after they had gained elementary qualifications in quality assurance. Suppliers reported pleasure with the new reliability, consistency and quality and orders rocketed by 20%. The owner was overjoyed and I was handsomely rewarded.

There are many different ways that quality can be assured and controlled. Nowadays, when customers can easily post negative reviews on a variety of social media platforms, companies know that if the quality of the service they are providing to their customers is poor, their business can suffer considerably. Giving examples of ensuring quality in customer service, especially complaints handling, often grabs the attention of employers.

Example 2 :

When I began working for a small mail-order company, I was shocked at the level of customer service. The products offered were of decent quality but the service was poor, the owner believing that the internet was a bottomless pit of potential customers and that the 'professional moaners' should go elsewhere.

After analysing the situation, **I created a customer care culture**, putting the quality of customer service first. **I issued mission and values statements**, setting basic standards. After consulting with colleagues, I then consulted with customers by way of surveys to ascertain their expectations and needs. I also analysed all recent complaints and suggestions.

I organised staff training to improve both product knowledge, customer service and communication skills. Precise targets and standards having now been communicated, staff were monitored for quality (by observation, **mystery shoppers** and by software) on average response times, transaction times and ratio of ensuing complaints. The quality criteria included reliability, responsiveness, competence, approachability, courtesy, communication skill, credibility and adherence to values and policies. Good staff were rewarded, bad were weeded out.

My suggestion that the website be made more transparent over delivery times, VAT costs and company policies on refunds and exchanges was implemented.

The result was that I stopped the haemorrhage of customers, I achieved a 20% increase in customer satisfaction targets, a 15% increase in compliments, 10% increase in sales in first quarter , 10% increase in repeat sales, increased revenue by targeting sales to the customers' needs and an 85% reduction in complaints.

Example 3 - You started a job in a Goods Receipt Department. Faulty goods were being returned but there was no systematic method of recording the returns. *" If you can't measure something, you can't improve it."* You devised a Returns Checklist which included checking for shortage; loss; damaged goods; wrong goods; mistakenly delivered / unordered goods; wrong quantity, wrong size; wrong colour; wrong description; wrong reference number; wrong "In date/ Freshness label etc. You ensured that all breakages, shortages, mistakes and late deliveries were refused and the refusals were recorded and dated on the new Returns Checklist sheet. This not only assured quality in your department but also saved your employer around 5% , £20,000 per year in payments for faulty goods.

Example 4 – You noticed that a few links on your company's website were not working, which made your organisation look amateurish and were probably losing your company customers. You immediately notified the I.T department, who speedily rectified them.

Example 5 :

I once worked in a high-class, prestigious West End store. Cleanliness of the store was absolutely paramount to our business, brand and image. Unfortunately, we were frequently being let down by the non-attendance incidents of our cleaners, due to childrens' illnesses, transport strikes and for various other reasons.

I suggested having a "Drop Everything Staff List", which was a list of cleaners, who were willing to literally drop everything without notice when contacted on their "always-on" phones and race down to the store to deputise for the absentee. They would be paid at triple rate and their taxi-fare would be prepaid for them.

I also suggested that in future, we hired cleaners who lived locally within walking distance, who would be unaffected by transport strikes.

My ideas were adopted. The result was that whenever a cleaner phoned in unable to do that shift, a replacement was immediately found and the service to the customer suffered no loss of quality whatsoever, since we were able to open on time, spick and span as ever. I maintained quality by being proactive rather than reactive and was promoted for it.

Ways of adding value :

You can ensure a high quality of service by adding value to the service you provide. Some ways of doing this are : (1) Provide more convenience (2) Provide a swifter response (3) Provide an after-sales service or care.

For example, you provided a Saturday mornng service for customers unable to make weekdays. You provided an answer-machine service for call-backs for when you were very busy. You provided alternative contact details in your "Out of Office" email notification, so that those contacting you could be dealt with by someone else .

The Attention to Detail Competencies

The interviewer wants to be sure that you have a keen eye for detail, that you paid great attention to your work and that you controlled your errors.

- I double-checked the accuracy of my work using a structured checklist
- I had someone else check my work, if appropriate
- I measured everything at least twice. " Measure twice, cut once."
- I was careful, meticulous and thorough
- I continually sought to improve my accuracy
- I took pride in my work
- I had a zero tolerance policy to my own mistakes
- I prevented distractions to my work
- I took a ' Right-First-Time ' approach to my work
- I kept all relevant data, calendars, schedules handy
- I ensured data and equipment was updated regularly
- I took any important messages in writing
- I had any messages / numbers /unusual names repeated and spelled out
- I followed all procedures and standards

Attention to Detail Examples :

1. You worked on a till or did the petty cash. You were Miss Penny Perfect and won monthly shop awards for it.
2. You worked with figures and NEVER had any work returned to you for correction.
3. You carefully measured or weighed or calculated things. You fitted carpets. You measured wallpaper. You hate waste.
4. You cut lengths of valuable materials, such as tiles, regal velvet curtains, carpets.
5. You monitored instruments, dials, meters or gauges.
6. You checked, inspected and did quality control.
7. You recorded details perfectly. You entered data onto a spreadsheet or database.
8. You copied and scanned important legal documents or similar financial ones.
9. You arranged items, such as a collection of books/CDs in strict alphabetical order.
10. You catalogued and filed papers/books meticulously to British Library standards.
11. You processed information / data in order to balance the equation/ books.
12. You made a meticulous record of things.

13. You did stock ordering or stock control in a shop or warehouse.
14. You followed very strict guidelines, rules or procedures to the letter.
15. You took the minutes of your team meetings. You then checked the accuracy. You then emailed them to all who attended for review and further thoughts to be signed off as a true record. When done, you forwarded them to all relevant absentees and partners.

Example 6
John gave an example of how he worked in a call-centre which took emergency calls from people reporting gas leaks. He told how he had to enter names, totally accurate addresses including postcodes and totally accurate phone numbers. He then had to give out accurate instructions to the caller. He then had to despatch the emergency gas workers. He included getting the caller to repeat the address and phone numbers back to him and spell any unusual names. He was commended each year for his accuracy.

Example 7
You worked in a Customer Services Department in an office and you noticed that many of the problems revolved around the staff recording the customers' emails slightly incorrectly : the letter O was often mistakenly transcribed as the figure zero and the letter I was being written as the figure one. You suggested that everyone use the same phonetic alphabet when taking calls, to record the email and then to repeat the emails from the screen back to the customer. It was adopted and the error rate halved.

Example 8

You had computer programming as a hobby : if you typed even one comma or full stop incorrectly, the program wouldn't run, so attention to detail was crucial.

If you are school leaver and did the sciences, you can write how for example, your chemistry project was compromised if you had not assured the quality of the correct concentration of the ingredients . If you had not measured the powders / liquids exactly, you would have derived an erroneous result – or blown yourself up ! If you are a school leaver and did Sociology or Geography or Psychology, you can write how you had to ensure your statistics were solid or else your conclusions would have been invalid. Both of those examples illustrated the necessity to ensure quality in your work.

Competency 10 Delivering at Pace

" Delivering timely performance with energy; taking responsibility and responsibility for quality outcomes; working to agreed goals and dealing with challenges in a responsive and constructive way.

For leaders, it is building a performance culture to deliver outcomes; keeping a firm focus on priorities; addressing performing issues resolutely, fairly and promptly."

Delivering at Pace Competencies

Delivering at Pace. No, this does not mean running around like a paperboy delivering papers. Simply put, it means that you finish all your work, on time and to the expected standards. For this competency, you need to show that you understand the importance of taking responsibility for getting all your work done within the agreed timescales. How do you ensure that ? You must show that you appreciate the importance of PRIORITIZING, PLANNING, MONITORING YOUR WORKLOAD regularly and building in CONTINGENCY TIME . You must show the lengths you went to, in order to achieve your targets and meet your deadlines. You must show how you overcame setbacks and delays to your plans to fulfil your contracts with no loss of quality in your work.

- I prioritized my tasks into Urgent, Important and Routine.
- I planned ny work, setting my objectives using the SMARTER model – they were Specific , Measurable, Achievable, Realistic, Timebound, Evaluated, re-Evaluated
- I timetabled my work to meet deadlines in the most efficient way
- I took responsibility for meeting my targets and deadlines
- I anticipated potential pressure points, setbacks and delays by building contingency time into my schedule
- I reviewed and evaluated my work regularly
- I maintained a steady performance by keeping a sense of urgency and remaining focused on my objectives and deadlines
- I sought help with excessive work pressure, if needed
- I motivated myself to achieve the required outcomes
- I knew the status of my work at all times
- I used To-Do lists, diaries , calendars and alarms
- I used a Brought/Forward system to ensure nothing was missed
- I made cost effective use of all suitable resources available to me
- I regularly monitored my progress and objectives
- I usefully employed downtime such as waiting time, travel-time, etc.
- I tried to understand problems before they were a threat to delivery
- I dealt with setbacks in a calm, responsive and constructive way

- I renegotiated and extended / re-scheduled the deadline
- I carefully and appropriately delegated some work to others, if necessary
- I worked overtime / came in early/ stayed late / worked weekends.
- I worked at home, if necessary, to meet my targets or deadlines
- I enlisted the help of colleagues in return for future favours, if needed
- I remained focused on the desired outcomes
- I adopted a positive and thankful approach
- I was determined and resilient, breaking the task down into bite-size chunks, taking regular breaks and just not giving up.
- I prevented interruptions, eg keeping conversations short
- I prevented procrastination by staying focused on deadlines, by surrounding myself with motivational quotes and family photos and by breaking tasks down into bite-sized chunks and rewarding myself after each one.

Two cars have collided head on and a doctor, who happens to be driving by, stops to attend to the wounded. Should he dash in and treat the first victim he sees ? Should he treat the man he saw first , who is hobbling and who might have a broken ankle or should he treat the woman who can't breathe ? You know the answer.

The first thing you must do in any of your work is to stop for a moment and **TAKE STOCK** of the situation and not just charge headlong into it. You must **ASSESS THE WORKLOAD** for the day and your deadlines.
Then you must **PRIORITIZE** it into work which is Urgent, then work which is Important and then work which is just Routine. Obviously, you start doing the Urgent work first ! Prioritizing your work is such a vital component to efficiency and you MUST include it , both in the example you give and at your interview or you will fail. It is impossible to "Deliver at Pace" without it.
You must the **PLAN YOUR DAY** by assigning a certain amount of work per hour (eg you will process 5 applications per hour until 12 noon / manufacture 100 thingies per hour / phone 6 customers per hour, etc.). You will allow for unforeseen things such as interruptions with some **CONTINGENCY TIME** (perhaps 15 mins per day) and you will **MONITOR YOUR PROGRESS** at every hour of the clock (or half hour) and make approriate adjustments, if you are falling behind schedule.

13 examples of Delivering at pace

Example 1 :

A sudden job offer meant moving from my flat within 7 days or lose the job. It was full of my treasured belongings - books, CDs and furniture, which I had to pack or sell off. It meant hard decisions and a lot of work within a tight deadline.

Firstly, I queried the deadline, renegotiated it and had it extended by 2 days. I analysed all my jobs and the time and the resources I had available. I would have to contact all the utility companies, the council, the doctor, my landlord, the Royal Mail, the removal company and host of other parties too. I then planned my objectives using the SMARTER model (i.e. ensuring my objectives were Specific, Measurable, Achievable, Realistic, Timebound, Evaluated and Re-evaluated).

After careful thinking, I prioritized them into Urgent, Important and Non-urgent. I estimated a certain amount of time per task but I also built in contingency time to allow for delays and unknowns. I enlisted help from friends , who helped after work and all day on moving day and I carefully delegated appropriate tasks to them. I kept monitoring the work's progress and objectives on a daily basis using a B/F system in my diary and on an hourly basis. I donated half my stuff to charity and packed half.

The result was that I managed to move in time with only one or two small breakages. The whole experience reinforced for me the necessity of good planning.

Note how he included some of the all-important competency indicators of Delivering at Pace : ...planned my objectives using the SMARTER model ...... prioritized into Urgent, Important and Non-Urgent ......built contingency time .....reviewed and evaluated work regularly.....used a B/F system.........employed downtime.....prevented interruptions....... enlisted help........ carefully delegated.

Be sure to say you planned your work, monitored your progress often, had a system or two in place to ensure none was missed and that you prevented interruptions (perhaps by keeping conversations very short or by asking colleagues to keep social talk for the tea breaks , If working from home, you told friends not to bother you for a day or two and you turned off the phone).

Tell how you kept yourself motivated when faced with sudden difficulties - you renegotiated the deadline, or amount of work; you asked others for help; you delegated to the intern / work experience kid; you worked overtime, etc.

Example 2 :

> When studying for my NVQ3in Computing, I had no PC. I had to complete all the modules, gather the evidence and have it assessed within a tight 13-week timescale, all while sharing computers. I knew this would require good planning and self-discipline.
>
> I planned my objectives using the SMARTER model and prioritised the work. I allocated so many modules per week, using weekly and daily To-Do lists. I factored in an extra 10% contingency time, in case of sickness or delays. I booked a PC for the times I needed one for the first month and then set reminders for the rest.
>
> I used a B/F system in my pocket diary to ensure no uncompleted assignment was missed and I evaluated my progress each day and altered my plans, if needed.
>
> I worked steadily and consistently and kept my objective and deadline in mind at all times. I pre-empted distractions and interruptions by telling friends not to call me or visit at certain times; by keeping conversations brief; by turning off my phone and by not answering my door, if needed.
>
> I prevented procrastination by breaking difficult modules down into smaller, more manageable chunks and by reminding myself of the potential reward and consequences of failure.
>
> The outcome was that, due to good planning, frequent monitoring, awareness of deadlines and self-discipline, I comfortably completed all the modules , had them assessed on time and I gained my desired qualification.

Example 3 : You completed an essay or coursework by a certain date

Example 4 : You completed work for a customer by a set date, perhaps serviced or repaired a car

Example 5 : You completed research and submitted your report , which had been commissioned by your boss on time

Example 6 : You met your sales targets in order to meet your commission

Example 7 : You met your production targets to receive your pay – so any burgers cooked per hour or items packed into a box

Example 8 : You learned your lines in time for a play or musical

Example 9 : You learned a piece of music for a recital or gig

Example 10 : You organised a function, kids' party, funeral, fete or wedding

Example 11: You worked through your lunch or weekend to meet your deadline

Example 12 : You did a college course, submitting several assignments and projects on time, while bringing up kids or while coping with a bereavement.

You can perhaps say how you planned your time to accommodate study, childcare and part-time work and achieved your objective within the set timeframe. Perhaps your example could be one of how you planned and prioritised the use of your family resources to clear sudden, unforeseen debts within a certain time .

Example 13 : You had a small company of computer programmers. You were planning to launch a new game when you read that a competitor was about to bring out a similar one just before your own. You asked your team if they would postpone their holidays and all work longer to get the project completed ahead of schedule. They did and you delived what proved to be a highly profitable product.

Chapter 7 Competency Options tests

The application process for certain jobs involves your having to complete a Competency Options Test as the next stage of your recruitment. In this, you are given a situation and told to rank four given responses which most closely matched the behaviour you exhibited in that situation.

For example, in a CUSTOMER SERVICES situation, you are told to think of a time when you dealt with a customer who was very demanding in terms of the time, advice and amount of help they wanted from you. You are told to rank these four responses in order from 1 to 4, with 1 being the response you took and 4 being the least likely you would have taken :

A ... I began with the intention of treating everyone equally but I found that I liked some people more than others and I admit that I was more likely to help those more.

B ... I can't pretend that I treated everyone the same. The ones who were undeserving and had bad attitudes got the bare service from me.

C ... I tried to be always fair and helpful but I must admit that how I treated people varied with how they treated me and how I felt on the day.

D ... I ensured that I was as fair as could be and that everyone received the same treatment , no matter how I felt personally.

The best way to tackle these is to firstly look for the WORST response : in other words, the action that you would certainly NOT have taken and to mark it as number 4. So here, I think you will agree that the poorest example of delivering customer service is option B. Naturally, someone working in a customer service role cannot decide to give the " bare service" to their customers, just because the customers are being demanding or " undeserving " !

The next step is to identify the response that you would have taken. Here, it is option D. So, you mark that as number 1. You gave your best service to every customer, regardless of how difficult and demanding they were.

That is the strategy that you must always adopt : firstly identify the worst response because usually it is the easiest to decide and assign it to number 4. Then secondly, identify the best response and assign it to number 1. The remaining two options usually have only a very subtle difference between them and it is not too important in which order you place these. I would assign the second best response to A and the third to C. Final answer ....1-D, 2-A, 3-C, 4-B.

Another example ...a TEAMWORK test. You worked in a team and are told to rank these in order.

A ... When I worked with others, I valued the differences between us and that each person had something different to contribute.

B ... I found it difficult working with people who were different from me because you need people with more similarities than differences.

C ... I appreciate that people were entitled to be different from me and I tried to adjust to their different ways.

D ... I was quite uncomfortable if they were different from me and found it difficult to adjust to their different ways of thinking.

Again, follow the strategy .. look for the WORST option.......look for what you would NOT have done or said and mark that as number 4 ......

I think you will agree that the worst option has to be the last one . Now, look for the best one and mark it as number 1 .... I think you will agree that it has to be the first one in the list above : he " valued " the differences, whereas the third option only tried to adjust . I would now suggest that C is better than B and so C comes second.. Final answer = 1-A, 2-C,3-B, D-4.

Another example ....A test of ACCURACY ....You had to maintain accuracy in your work.

A ... I didn't check my work, as people were generally satisfied with it.

B - I spent almost as much time checking my time as I did doing it.

C - I checked those parts where errors could most easily creep in.

D ... I always checked my work , though as I grew in experience and confidence, I was able to spend less and less time on this.

Following the strategy, you look for the worst option and assign it to number 4. Then find the best option, that is, the one that you actually did and assign that to option number 1. Then decide the better of the remaining two and assign it to number 2.

Final answer is 1-D, 2-C, 3-B, 4-A

A is clearly the worst. It shows idleness, complacency and arrogance. B is the next worst . At least this person checks their wok but the employer would not recruit someone so incompetent. Of the remaining two, C is the poorer because errors can creep into any area of our work, not just the parts we expect.

The clever way to tackle these is to do them with friends and to share your thoughts. Two heads are better than one and five heads are better than two.

Don't fuss too much about the inner answers. It is the first and last in the ranks that you must get right.

Finally, before you submit your answers, recheck that you have written them in the correct order. It is VERY easy to record them incorrectly.

Chapter 8 After the interview and beyond

If you don't get that particular job

The secret in getting a good job is knowing the right thing to do, doing it and persisting in doing it until you are successful. When you have been rejected for a position, it can be for many reasons. You might have demonstrated your competencies perfectly but the employer felt that you would not fit into the culture of his company or that team for whatever reason. Sometimes, an employer will withdraw a vacancy after the interviews. It does happen . It could be that you were considered excellent but one candidate had slightly more experience than you. It is common for six candidates to be invited for an interview . Four might have scored less than 80 %. You might have scored 96 % but the winner scored 96.5%. Since you don't know how close you came to landing that job, you will feel that you are a failure and that you will never master these competency interviews and that you will never get the job you want. Sadly, this is what we tend to do. We think the worst. We catastrophise.

Examine how you performed and be honest. If you felt that you performed badly on any examples, ask yourself why. Did you need better examples ? Did you need more examples ? Did you need more practice ? If you were prodded for more details, were you able to give the specific detail that was wanted ?

What is important is that you move on and persist

By constructing an Experiences Autobiography, you are doing the right thing. By constructing and learning your scripts according to the model I have given, you are giving the employer examples of the key indicators of the competencies he is seeking. You are doing the right thing and on the right track. The final unit is for you to show perseverance. You will succeed if you persevere. The formula works and you will win when the conditions and time are right. Do not confine yourself to only applying for Civil Service or Local Government (Council) jobs. The competition is fierce. Apply for many other jobs too. You will need my other book, which details other competencies not given in this book. It also gives many examples for those.

What also counts is the time and effort you have expended in remembering all your experiences. Go back through your Autobiography and cross-check it with the key indicators given in chapters 7 and 8 and examples suggested underneath them. If you have very few experiences and examples and are really desperate, think of experiences of your brothers and sisters and friends.

Keep updating your Experiences Autobiography !

You must constantly keep adding to your Autobiography with examples of your behaviours. If you are currently working, stay alert to how you are contributing to your team for examples of Teamwork. If you work in a Customer Services environment, record examples of how you have delivered excellent service and how maybe dealt with demanding customers and complaints. **Simply spend 10 or 15 minutes at the end of each working day remembering and recording what you did that day**. It's easy if you travel by train or bus to jot it down in your diary or record it into your phone or mp3 voice recorder. Make it a daily habit of forcing yourself to briefly skim through all the competencies and **note down any examples**. Then some time later, you can expand them into scripts. **I cannot emphasise this enough.**

When you get the job - and you will, sooner or later - when you get that email or letter and you have calmed down after all the excitement, Congratulations ! Go out and buy yourself a treat ...... a nice ice-cream or some sweets or a nice fruit drink ! **Finally....... If you bought this book on Amazon......**If you have found this book helpful and you bought it on Amazon, PLEASE be so kind and give it a good rating. You might also wish to buy another copy to give to someone you know, who is looking for work or to change their job. **You might also wish to buy some of my other books. Search Amazon for 'Mike New'**

Thank you. I wish you good luck and all good things in life.

Mike

33577558R00051

Printed in Poland
by Amazon Fulfillment
Poland Sp. z o.o., Wrocław